THE EVOLUTION OF THE
PASSENGER SHIP

CHRIS FRAME AND RACHELLE CROSS

The History Press

For Rob Henderson

*For your decades-long dedication and
commitment to the preservation of maritime
history and your unwavering support
for us over the last decade.*

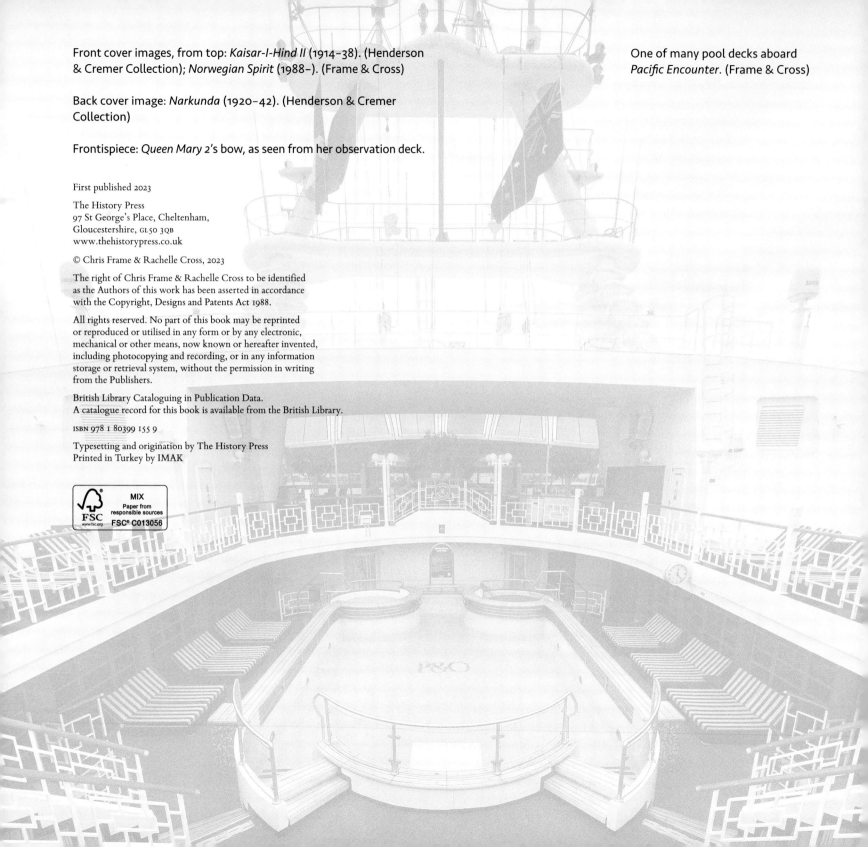

Front cover images, from top: *Kaisar-I-Hind II* (1914–38). (Henderson & Cremer Collection); *Norwegian Spirit* (1988–). (Frame & Cross)

Back cover image: *Narkunda* (1920–42). (Henderson & Cremer Collection)

Frontispiece: *Queen Mary 2*'s bow, as seen from her observation deck.

One of many pool decks aboard *Pacific Encounter*. (Frame & Cross)

First published 2023

The History Press
97 St George's Place, Cheltenham,
Gloucestershire, GL50 3QB
www.thehistorypress.co.uk

British Library Cataloguing in Publication Data.
A catalogue record for this book is available from the British Library.

ISBN 978 1 80399 155 9

Typesetting and origination by The History Press
Printed in Turkey by IMAK

FSC MIX
Paper from responsible sources
www.fsc.org FSC® C013056

CONTENTS

Acknowledgements   6

Foreword by Dr Stephen Payne OBE   8

1   Travel by Sail   11

2   The First Steamships   19

3   Creature Comforts   25

4   Changing the Shape of the World   35

5   Building for Purpose   47

6   Bigger, Better, Stronger   57

7   Bad Times and Good Times   71

8   Not Their Intended Use   87

9   Last Age of the Liner   121

10   This Changes Everything   131

11   Rise of the Cruise Ships   147

12   Popular Culture   155

13   The Cruising Boom   167

14   Collapse and Resurrection   181

Bibliography   189

About Chris and Rachelle   192

ACKNOWLEDGEMENTS

Our objective in writing this book was to take you on a journey through the remarkable story of the passenger ship. The topic is huge, and this is by no means an exhaustive history. Rather, it is our hope that this book provides you with an overview of some of the most important evolutions that had an impact on the passenger ship.

It is these changes that saw passenger ships grow from small wooden vessels, reliant on oars or the wind, to the massive cruise ships we see today. It allowed them to make such a significant impact on our world, and the lives of countless people.

When we first decided to write this book, we knew that it would be a mammoth undertaking, and it wouldn't have been possible without the help and support of some fantastic people.

We'd like to thank everyone who helped make this book a reality.

A special thanks goes to:

Dr Stephen Payne for writing the foreword, conversations and insight into passenger shipping design, and photographic support.

Rob Henderson and Doug Cremer for access to the remarkable historic archive that they have spent a lifetime preserving.

Our thanks to a generous group of photographic contributors whose photography and collections have helped bring this story to life: Alison Morton, Andrew Sassoli-Walker, Bill Miller, Colin Hargreaves, Commodore R.W. Warwick, George Frame, Luke Morrison, Michael W. Pocock, Peter Knego, Rob Lightbody, Russell Smith and Vicki Cross.

A huge thanks to our commissioning editor Amy Rigg, who has been our publishing partner since our first book, as well as to Rebecca Newton, Martin Latham, Jemma Cox and the whole team at The History Press, and our families and friends for supporting us.

Departure. The spectacle of a departing ocean liner was often celebrated by the throwing of streamers, as passengers farewelled their loved ones on the pier. (Henderson & Cremer Collection)

FOREWORD

The evolution of the passenger ship is a fascinating and diverse subject, which encompasses layout design, on-board technologies and services offered. On the macro sense, a look at the evolutionary transition of Cunard's transatlantic liners spanning *Britannia* (1840), *Campania* (1893), *Mauretania* (1907), *Queen Mary* (1936), *Queen Elizabeth* (1940), *Queen Elizabeth 2* (1969) and finally *Queen Mary 2* (2004) provides much insight.

Within the forty years separating *Britannia* and *Campania*, paddle wheels had given way to twin-screw propellers, wooden hulls had transitioned to iron and then steel, and the somewhat meagre accommodation arrangements had improved noticeably. However, the forthcoming *Mauretania* would be a quantum leap in technology for the quest of increased speed, with steam reciprocating engines being replaced by steam turbines, albeit at a huge increase in operating costs that required an operating subsidy and full use of the axiom of economy of scale.

Mauretania had to accommodate a large number of passengers to make her economically viable and the scale of her accommodations could rightly enable her, along with her sister *Lusitania*, to be classed as the grandest hotel on the North Atlantic. All points taken, *Mauretania* and *Lusitania* were revolutionary, taking evolution several steps further.

Moving on twenty-nine years, the much loved *Queen Mary*, considered by many as *the* archetypal ocean liner, was perhaps less evolutionary than her predecessors. She did employ geared steam turbines rather than the direct drive type fitted on *Mauretania*, which improved economy, her accommodations were more commodious and embraced the art deco movement of the day, but in essence, *Queen Mary* was very conservative.

Four years later, *Queen Elizabeth*, often misquoted as a sister to *Queen Mary*, was altogether more evolutionary. In essence, she benefitted much from a Cunard official making a clandestine voyage on the French Line *Normandie* and reporting back improvements made on that ship. The consolidation of air exhausts and intakes, as on *Normandie*, grouping them within the funnel bases and eliminating the forest of vents and cowls, led to a massive improvement in layout and greatly reduced the maintenance effort required to service them. Halving the number of boilers led to only two and not three funnels, which released more space to the accommodation. Funnels were self-supporting, negating the multiplicity of guy wires that cluttered the upper decks on the *Mary*. *Elizabeth*'s flat forecastle without the well deck of her sibling increased accommodation volume and improved her seakeeping, as the well deck momentarily trapped green seas, leading to transitional stability loss. All in all, *Queen Elizabeth* was by far the more superior ship compared with *Queen Mary* but for some reason she's never captured the public's imagination as the *Mary* has done throughout her existence.

Twenty-nine years later *Queen Elizabeth 2* (*QE2*) came on the scene, and she was a complete game changer, another revolutionary evolution. Somewhat smaller than her illustrious predecessors, the latest technology of geared turbines and oversized boilers enabled the ship to offer full en suite facilities and more space per passenger than those ships. Out went polished brass and woodwork, in came chrome and plastic and 1960s pop chic.

Continuously metamorphosing, *QE2* would sail for thirty-nine years before being retired in 2008. In 2004 *Queen Mary 2* entered service, building on *QE2*'s features while maximising the cruising phenomenon of balcony cabins. The transatlantic liner had come a long way since *Britannia*, but everything that had been learned in the intervening period was incorporated into her design and operation.

Let's now briefly consider the micro evolutionary process of a trio of ships. Orient Line's post-war trio of passenger-cargo ships (*Orcades* 1949, *Oronsay* 1951 and *Orsova* 1954) evolved from the pre-war designs of *Orion* (1935) and *Orcades* (1937). Although the accommodation layout dispositions of first and tourist classes was similar between the pre- and post-war ships, the latter presented an altogether more radical profile with the bridge moved aft towards the funnel, providing space for a semi-enclosed games arena.

It would have been easy for Orient to have simply repeated the design of *Orcades* for the second ship, but major improvements were introduced that provided tourist class with an outdoor swimming pool and lido café. However, the disposition of hatch trunks continued to greatly compromise the layout of the tourist public spaces and this situation was much improved with the

Queen Mary 2 (2004–). The under-construction *Queen Mary 2*'s forward superstructure, showing the welding joints used to hold the ship together. (Dr Stephen Payne)

Queen Mary 2 (2004–). The enclosed bridge structure aboard *QM2* was designed to resemble that aboard *QE2*, while the detailing on the forward superstructure is a nod to the original *Queen Mary*. (Frame & Cross)

arrangements on *Orsova*. This latter ship was the most technologically advanced of the three with three large boilers rather than four smaller ones, an all-welded hull and easily cleanable and maintainable Formica- and vinyl-clad accommodation interiors. And yet, with all these assets, this fine ship barely remained in service for twenty years before succumbing to the scrapper's torch.

The sad fact was that *Orsova*, and her sisters, rapidly became simply outmoded and uneconomical. Steam turbine propulsion was hopelessly inefficient in the fuel crisis of the early 1970s, the two-class configuration and the many non-facility cabins became a burden, while commodious unused cargo space was a real liability to efficiency. The era of the purpose-built cruise ship had arrived.

Enough of my analysis, maritime aficionados Rachelle and Chris have looked further into the evolution of the passenger liner in this excellent book full of narrative and illustrations. My advice is to find your favourite spot on board your favourite ship, maybe the quiet corner of a lounge or shaded spot on deck, and cast off and set sail on an insightful adventure learning about how passenger ships evolved. Bon voyage!

Dr Stephen M. Payne OBE
Past President, The Royal Institution of Naval Architects
Designer Cunard Line *Queen Mary 2*

1

TRAVEL BY SAIL

There are few chapters of human history where ships don't play a central role. From the dawn of civilisation to recent global events, ships have been central to human development, movement, commerce and politics.

Record keeping in ancient times was largely oral and few written records have survived the passage of time, though an exception to this can be found from ancient Egypt. With the Nile playing a vital role in Egyptian development, it is little wonder that ships played a key role in Egypt's early rise.

As early as 4,000 BCE, ships were used to move goods, crops and people between settlements and cities. These early vessels were miniscule by today's standards. More akin to small boats than giant passenger liners, the Egyptian ships were powered by muscle, with oars being a central feature to control their movement in river waters.

Throughout the era of the Ancient Egyptian Empire, these small boats developed in both size and structure. Progress in the development of sturdier ships allowed pioneering sailors to wander into the Mediterranean Sea, attaching crude sails to wooden masts to offer a boost in power aided by the wind. This must have offered great relief to rowers, who, until then, had provided shipping propulsion.

Travelling in open sea proved to be a vastly different challenge than rowing in a river. Far from the safety of the riverbank, mastering wind power became essential for voyagers who wished to explore or establish trade connections with other civilisations.

While rowing was still utilised, especially in the close confines of ancient ports, journey by sail allowed early navigators to set their sights beyond the horizon. Early successes from Egyptian ports included voyages to Crete and coastal exploration along the African Mediterranean coast.

The Khufu Ship. Shipping was an integral part of Ancient Egypt and this original example is from around 2500 BCE. Known as a solar barge, it spans 43.4m long. It was recovered from the Great Pyramid of Giza in 1954. (Frame & Cross)

The Nile. The earliest records of shipping refer to boats transporting goods and people along the Nile. (Frame & Cross)

A tree brought from Punt. The ancient Egyptians ventured beyond their own borders. An expedition by Hatshepsut to Punt (likely on the Red Sea) brought items back to Egypt. (Frame & Cross)

In other parts of the world, boats and rafts were being used to explore and settle new lands. Despite utilising vessels that would be considered small by today's standards, they still managed to transit open ocean. This method of transportation allowed the Polynesian Islands to be settled roughly 4,000 BCE and the Caribbean islands sometime around 3,500 BCE.

As the Egyptian sailors ventured further into the Mediterranean, neighbouring civilisations took notice, and ships became a common sight among Mediterranean nations. Almost as quickly, ships became militarised, as these civilisations sought to ensure both security and conquest by way of the sea.

In these early days, ship designs were experimented with, creating traits that would have long-lasting implications for future shipbuilders.

Militarised ships began to prioritise wartime capability in the primary design. This included building ships for speed and manoeuvrability, achieved through designing smaller, narrow-beamed vessels that took advantage of both wind power and oars.

And from the early days of naval shipbuilding, the need for human transports was ever present, as the movement of soldiers was essential. Early navies pioneered the development of large cargo transports, which were generally an evolution of the slower, bulk carriers that had become increasingly common sights between the Mediterranean trading ports.

The design of trade or cargo ships prioritised stability over speed, with an emphasis on ensuring heavily laden vessels could remain afloat in all weather conditions, regardless of the ferocity of the seas.

As time passed, larger wooden-hulled ships became familiar sights across the globe. By the eighth century, Arabian traders had reached China and Chinese traders had explored as far as what is now Ethiopia and Somalia. Chinese shipbuilders had also developed fleets of wooden-hulled sailing junks that plied the South China Sea from the sixth century CE, providing trade and commerce opportunities for local merchants.

In CE 985 Bjarni Herjólfsson led a Norse expedition to Greenland. Bad weather blew them off course and it is believed that they sighted America on this voyage. It would be over five hundred years before Christopher Columbus 'discovered' the Americas in 1492.

Endeavour replica (1994–). Early explorers spent months at sea while searching for new lands. The original *Endeavour* was a 29.77m-long collier that had been converted to a bark. It was commanded by Lt James Cook. (Frame & Cross)

Rudder. The rudder was exposed on many of the early ships, particularly when the design included a counter stern. (Frame & Cross)

Sailing masts. The demand for wood to create masts led to the formation of a thriving mast trade. Due to their size, masts were made from some of the oldest and tallest trees. Unfortunately, this led to mass deforestation, leading to significant environmental impacts. (Frame & Cross)

Opposite: Bowsprit of *Leeuwin II* (1986–). The bowsprit is a spar that points forward from the bow of the ship. On sailing ships the bowsprit is used as an anchor point for the forward sails. (Frame & Cross)

In 1519 an expedition led by Ferdinand Magellan departed Seville, Spain. Magellan, along with many of the crew, died during the journey. It was completed under the command of Juan Sebastián Elcano. The journey was fraught with challenges, including a lack of knowledge about the route they were attempting. Of the five ships that departed, only one completed the full journey.

As the European empires continued to explore and colonise foreign lands, they built ships to carry settlers to all corners of the globe. These ships differed depending on where they were built and their intended purpose. Multiple styles of ships were used on these long-duration voyages, even when travelling to the same destination.

For example, the First Fleet of 1788 that commenced the British settlement of what is now Australia consisted of eleven ships, with varying purposes. There were two naval vessels, three supply and food transport ships and six ships that transported passengers, most of whom had not elected to take the voyage but were rather being transported as convicts.

With the establishment of new settlements and outposts came a need to provide a link back to Europe. This encouraged the development of commercial ventures as well as the establishment of corporations to manage the supply chains. Port cities became larger and more complex, as infrastructure was built to support the increase in trade. Many of the world's largest cities were built on waterways because of the importance of ocean trade.

The influx of funding and financing allowed for the development of passenger ships, and during this age of sail there were several design traits that became familiar across the various ship designs.

As the ships grew, so did their components, which were given common names to identify the various parts of a vessel, regardless of its type. The ship was built with a wooden skeletal structure attached to a central keel, while wooden masts made from ancient trees were essential to ensure sails could be hoisted. The central mast was referred to as the mainmast, while a forward-facing spar at the bow became known as the bowsprit.

Rudders were used for steering the ship, while anchors were developed to hold the ship in place when stopped.

Many European ships had a raised forward deck, commonly referred to as a forecastle, so raised as to offer a good vantage point to defend the vessel from attackers, as well as offering some shelter from inclement seas for those working on the main deck.

This arrangement was mirrored at the stern with an aftercastle deck. As ships continued to grow, the aftercastle gave way to a quarter deck. This space housed officers and was usually where the ship's steering and navigation was managed.

Polynesian voyaging canoes often had twin hulls, rather like modern catamarans, making them more stable. The Russian koch, which was used for Arctic exploration, had additional skin planking, and djongs, used by Javanese people, were reportedly very strong due to additional planking being laid over the ships as the wood beneath became old.

Even though these ships had common components, this didn't mean that they were identical in appearance. There were many variations in hull design, with various hydrodynamic shapes pioneered and tested during the centuries of sail. The number of masts and sails that a ship carried, as well as its steering mechanism, also varied between regions and the purpose of the ship.

Both hull design and sail arrangement were used to describe different types of ships, with names such as clipper, schooner, barque/bark and frigate all being used.

By the eighteenth century there were countless ships carrying passengers to destinations around the world, but the experience was quite different to modern-day transportation. The scheduling of most departures was based on when the ship had enough passengers and cargo booked to justify the expense of the voyage.

In 1818 the Black Ball Line, at that time known as the Wright, Thompson, Marshall, & Thompson Line, introduced a revolutionary concept to transatlantic shipping: regular scheduled departures, regardless of if the ship was full or not. The new concept of departing on a specific day of each month proved very popular with merchants, who were willing to pay extra for a guaranteed departure date.

Their first four ships to undertake the scheduled departure service were all sailing packets of around 400 tons. Named *James Monroe*, *Amity*, *Pacific* and *Courier*, they carried both cargo and passengers. It could be said that these ships revolutionised the shipping industry.

Red Star Line followed suit in 1821, with other shipping lines copying the concept as time went on. Of course, despite a regular departure date, the arrival date was changeable and based on sea and weather conditions. The westbound crossing was often much longer than the eastbound, with an average of twenty-five days for the eastbound voyage in 1818 and forty-three days westbound, due to the challenges of sailing against the Gulf Stream.

But the golden age for sail was already drawing to a close. Experimental steamships were being launched, offering the potential of a faster crossing. Though steamships were still in their infancy, the world was beginning to change, and shipping companies needed to adapt to what was soon to be a vastly different operating environment.

Many shipping companies chose to invest in the new technology, while also maintaining and expanding their more traditional fleets. The Orient Line is best remembered for its express steamship services between the United Kingdom and Australia, however its origins were in the age of sail.

The organisation's founding family, the Thomsons, had been involved in sailing ship transport since 1797. By the nineteenth century one of its leaders was a young man named James Anderson. Anderson came from a Scottish family, whose maritime links dated back to the 1560s.

Under the direction of Anderson, the line, then known as James Thomson & Co., established their first links with Australia and New Zealand in 1850. Despite steamships already gaining popularity, this pioneering voyage was undertaken by the sailing packet *Charlotte Jane*. It proved successful, with 1,699 bales of wool and 5,000 hides carried back to the United Kingdom.

This voyage proved the viability of long-duration cargo services to Australia and encouraged the organisation to commission a clipper ship in 1853. At 56m (183.7ft) long and with a beam of 9.66m (31.6ft), *Orient* was small by today's standards and spent the first years of her service career under requisition in the Crimean War.

Released from requisition in 1856, the ship undertook five successful voyages to Australia, encouraging James Thomson & Co., to order a new vessel named *Murray*. The arrival of this ship in 1861 prompted the line to market their services as 'the Orient Line of Clipper Ships'.

The firm famously opted to retain their fully sail-powered fleet well into the early era of the steamship and they were among the most notable operators of iconic sailing ship designs, including the Blackwall frigate.

This type of ship replaced many of the older sailing ships operated by British companies and was designed specifically to capture the fast trade winds in the era before the opening of the Suez Canal. The design made these ships ideal for the Australian and Indian trade. Orient Line's 1,431-ton *Agamemnon* was one such example and was built in 1855 by R. & H. Green.

The R. & J. Craig of Glasgow-owned *County of Peebles* is cited as the first four-masted, fully rigged, iron-hulled ship. It entered service in 1875 and replaced the wooden hulls of traditional shipbuilding with iron plating. There were numerous iron-hulled sailing ships designed, including the windjammers, which were large and fast enough to compete with the early steamships.

Several of these remarkable iron-hulled sailing ships still exist, including the USS *Constitution* and the *James Craig*. The former is a US navy vessel and remains commissioned, while the latter was built in 1874 as a cargo carrier and still sails today as part of the Sydney Heritage Fleet.

Another example is the *Star of India*. Originally built in 1863 as the *Euterpe*, she was used in the 1870s as an immigration ship sailing between the United Kingdom and New Zealand, a service she performed for twenty-five years, well into the age of steam.

Amsterdam replica (1985–). Het Scheepvaartmuseum is the home of the replica of the Dutch east Indiaman *Amsterdam*. The original ship sank on its first voyage to Batavia (Jakarta) in 1749. (Frame & Cross)

James Craig (1874–). *James Craig* is an iron-hulled barque that became obsolete when the steamships took the majority of ocean trade. Scuttled in 1932, the ship was restored beginning in 1972. (Frame & Cross)

2

THE FIRST STEAMSHIPS

Rudimentary steam engines have been recorded as far back as the first century CE, but it wasn't until the 1700s that steam engines really began to show promise as a way to generate motive power at scale.

Throughout the 1700s various engineers worked on developing the steam engine, making incremental improvements. One of the best known was James Watt, whose 1776 steam engine would be used on what is often held to be the first commercially successful passenger steamboat.

Though the first commercially viable service did not commence until 1807, there were several earlier steamboat services. These included the *Palmipède* in 1776, which was developed by Claude-François-Dorothée and sailed on the Doubs River for several weeks.

Fourteen years later, John Fitch and Henry Voigt built a steamboat in America, to run on the Delaware River. The steam engine designed by the pair powered oars that propelled the boat in a similar way to rowing. Though this early service was successful in a mechanical sense, financial difficulties meant that the venture failed.

The 1807 import of the Watt steam engine to America advanced steamboat development further. Launched in 1807, the *North River Steamboat*, otherwise known as *Clermont*, ran on the Hudson River. Operated by Robert Fulton, this service was the first to be considered a commercial success. The *Clermont* employed rudimentary paddle wheels for propulsion.

In the early years, steamboats were not able to undertake long voyages. They were mostly employed over short distances, traversing rivers or lakes, or on coastal voyages. In 1809, the first ever steam-powered, seagoing voyage was made by the *Phoenix*.

Built in 1807 in New York, *Phoenix* was a paddle steamer and designed for river journeys. In 1809 she was repositioned to Philadelphia, undertaking the voyage by sea. Though not an easy journey, the ship arrived and was able to commence trading from her new port.

Between 1816 and 1818 the first deep-water expeditions by steamship took place. These crossings were short, transiting the English Channel, but they were soon to be overshadowed by a much longer deep-water venture.

In 1819 the *Savannah* crossed the Atlantic, using steam power for part of her journey. *Savannah* was originally intended to be a wooden-hulled sailing packet, however the ship was purchased during her construction at the Frickett & Corkett yards in New York. She was converted at the request of her new owner to include steam-powered, side-driven paddle wheels.

With her new configuration, *Savannah* departed Savannah, Georgia, on 22 May 1819 under steam power. Throughout her journey her engines were used sporadically, operating under sail power for the majority of her voyage. Despite running out of coal during the voyage and arriving under wind power alone, she nonetheless made headlines in Liverpool and her home port when she arrived, the first ship to cross the Atlantic using steam power.

Savannah did not have a long service career as a steamship. Financial difficulties for her owners led to the sale of the vessel in 1820, with the ship's engine and paddle wheels being removed and sold back to their builders. *Savannah* re-entered service as a sailing packet, remaining in this role until it wrecked in 1821.

The next steamship to cross the Atlantic was the *Curaçao*, a Dutch-owned vessel, built in Dover. She departed Hellevoetsluis, Netherlands, on 26 April 1827 and made way to Paramaribo, Suriname, in twenty-eight days. Like *Savannah*, she did not enjoy a long service career, though she did make several crossings of the Atlantic under steam.

The next passenger ship of note to cross the Atlantic using steam power for at least part of the journey was the *Royal William*. Built for the Quebec and Halifax Steam Navigation Company, she was launched in 1831.

The Quebec and Halifax Steam Navigation Company folded in 1833 and the ship was purchased by six of the mortgage holders. The decision was made to sell the ship in England and the *Royal William* made the Atlantic crossing in 1833. This crossing was notable for several reasons. Firstly, the ship made way under steam power for the whole of the journey, though there were refuelling stops, and the voyage was augmented by sail when her boilers required cleaning after 'salting up' with sea water.

The other notable outcome of the *Royal William*'s crossing was that several of the original investors, including Samuel Cunard, saw at first-hand the success of the steam-powered Atlantic crossing.

While the distances involved made the Atlantic crossing the most impressive display of the evolving steam technology, it was also being utilised on many other routes. And with many varied operators.

One such service was run by the Peninsular Steam Navigation Company (PSN. Co., which would later become P&O). Under the direction of its founders Arthur Anderson and Brodie McGhie Wilcox, from 1835 the company operated the *William Fawcett* on their mail service to the Iberian Peninsula. *William Fawcett* was a 206-ton, steam-powered paddle ship, chartered from the Dublin & London Steam Packet Company.

PSN. Co. quickly expanded their service, adding *Royal Tar* and *Jupiter* and then *Iberia*, *Braganza* and *Liverpool*. In 1837 PSN. Co. was awarded a British government contract to carry mails to the Iberian Peninsula.

The mail contract gave them the financial stability to further expand their service, with five ships initially employed on this route. The PSN. Co. fleet included the 932-ton *Don Juan*, which was touted as one of the world's largest steamships at the time.

While steamships had proven their ability to cross oceans, there had yet to be a direct, non-stop, long-distance crossing of an ocean completed entirely under steam propulsion. In fact, there was a prevailing theory among the European scientific and engineering communities that water resistance on the hull of a steamship directly impacted its performance. Although accurate, the theory popularised by Dionysius Lardner went a step further, claiming that the impact of water resistance had an insurmountable correlating effect on fuel consumption.

In short, the larger the ship, the more water resistance. The more water resistance, the more coal it would need. The more coal carried, the larger the ship had to be to carry said coal. This never-ending cycle, it was theorised, would limit the size of a steamer capable of operating solely under steam to 800 tons – too small to carry enough fuel to undertake long deep-water crossings.

Isambard Kingdom Brunel did not subscribe to this popularised theory. Already a successful engineer, Brunel had been involved in building the tunnel under the Thames, designing a number of bridges and was heavily involved in the G.W.R. (Great Western Railway), where he became chief engineer.

He wanted to expand the rail network across the Atlantic, so he set his mind to how that could be done. In 1836, Brunel and a group of Bristol investors formed the Great Western Steamship Company, and that same year the *Great Western* was laid down in Bristol at the Patterson & Mercer shipyard. She was launched in 1837 and during fitting out was given two side-lever steam engines. Her maiden voyage departed Bristol on 8 April 1838, having been delayed due to a fire in the engine room and Brunel being injured in a fall.

The steamship *Sirius* was a steam packet, and was chartered by rival company, the British and American Steam Navigation Company, to challenge *Great Western*'s attempt to be the first ship to cross the Atlantic using steam power the whole way. *Sirius* departed Cork on her first Atlantic crossing on 4 April. She had been refitted to add room for extra coal bunkers, but despite this ran low on coal during the journey, requiring the crew to burn other items to maintain steam.

Sirius arrived in New York on 22 April, and for a single day held the record for the fastest Atlantic crossing. *Great Western* arrived the next day, taking the record, having crossed the Atlantic in fourteen days. She still had 200 tons of coal on board.

The improvement of steamship technology was noticed not only by shipping entrepreneurs, but also by governments worldwide, who were eager to improve the reliability of both cargo and mail delivery. Transatlantic mails regularly took over a month to be carried between the United Kingdom and the United States, while both closer to home and further afield the situation was equally woeful.

One of the most significant mail contracts to be awarded in the early years of the steamship was for the transatlantic service. In November 1838 the British government put out a call for tenders to run the transatlantic mail service by steamship.

The winner would need to provide a solution for a fort-nightly delivery with a minimum weekly departure undertaken by a fleet of four vessels. Services were required to link the United Kingdom with the British colony of Nova Scotia, and the east coast of the United States.

In 1839 Nova Scotian entrepreneur Samuel Cunard travelled to the United Kingdom to submit a bid. Cunard was backed by a group of businessmen in the United Kingdom, including George Burns, James Burns, David McIver and Charles McIver. He was also supported by Robert Napier, a prominent naval architect.

The group, led by Samuel Cunard, bid for the tender and were successful over rivals, including the Great Western Steamship Co. To service the contract, Napier designed four paddle steamers, *Britannia*, *Caledonia*, *Acadia* and *Columbia*. The first of these ships, *Britannia*, was 63.09m (209ft) long, built

Sirius replica. A replica of *Sirius* appeared as the ship *Dog Star* in the 1939 movie, *Rulers of the Sea*. (Michael W. Pocock/ www.maritimequest.com)

of wood and was able to carry not only the mails but also 115 fare-paying passengers.

The British and North American Royal Mail Steam Packet Company (better known as Cunard's Line) service departed Liverpool, bound for Halifax, Nova Scotia, and then on to Boston. The journey took fourteen days and was completed at an average speed of 9 knots. Despite carrying enough coal for the journey, Cunard captains were instructed to use their sails whenever the winds were favourable.

Cunard's Line was able to achieve an evolution in ocean-going passenger transport. The line achieved this not because their ships were revolutionary in design, but because of the financial stability offered by the mail contract. This stability allowed the line to quickly introduce a fleet of four ships, enabling the Cunard service to commence regular frequent scheduled crossings.

Clockwise from above: *Great Britain* (1845–86). In addition to having steam engines, early steamships, such as Brunel's *Great Britain,* were also fully rigged for sail; Prior to the invention of refrigeration technology, ships carried livestock aboard to provide food. Animals would often share the same spaces as the passengers; The early steamships had no superstructure. There were often small deckhouses, but the passenger accommodation and public spaces were all located within the ship's hull. (Frame & Cross)

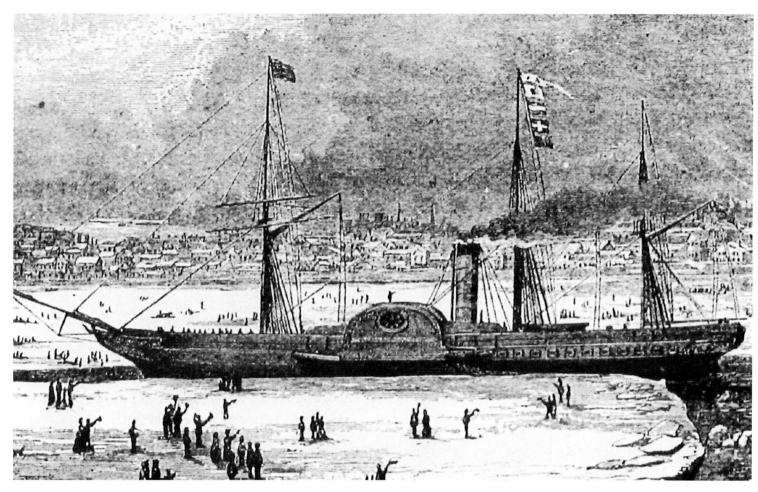

Britannia (1840–80). The first purpose-built steamship of the Cunard Line remained in Cunard service for nine years. The ship was much loved, with the people of Boston helping to free her when she became stuck in ice in the harbour. (Commodore R.W. Warwick. QE2: The Cunard Line Flagship Queen Elizabeth II)

Cunard Steamship Company Limited emblem. In 1879 the British and North American Royal Mail Steam Packet Company was reorganised and became officially known as the Cunard Steamship Company Limited. (Frame & Cross)

Samuel Cunard. A pioneer of transatlantic shipping, Sir Samuel Cunard was one of the founders of the Cunard Line. Here he is depicted aboard *QE2*, alongside his beloved paddle steamers in a mural by Peter Sutton. (Frame & Cross)

FROM FICTION TO FACT

The idea of a pleasure voyage was mooted at the dawn of the steamship era. British entrepreneur Arthur Anderson, who went on to gain fame for his role in establishing P&O, was one person to suggest the idea early on. Years before P&O's first pleasure cruise, Anderson dreamed up a concept of a long-duration pleasure voyage – not to sell tickets, but to sell newspapers.

Anderson's newspaper, the *Shetland Journal*, needed advertisers. Empty space in a newspaper gives the impression of there being little interest in the paper's columns, so to fill it Anderson used his imagination.

The result was an advertisement for a voyage aboard the steamer *Hyperborean*, on a voyage from Scallaway to Iceland. The voyage was completely fictitious, yet the description of the experience shares an uncanny resemblance to the modern cruise holiday.

This idea was a curiosity when it was published on 11 June 1836. It would take half a century before cruising would start to gain serious traction, and even longer before it revolutionised holiday travel.

3

CREATURE COMFORTS

Travelling by steamship was a luxury, though not in the way we would view luxuries today. The luxury of the steamship was largely the ability to undertake travel in a more timely manner, not the amenities on board. Steam services were primarily designed for the carriage of mails and cargo. While there was a growing number of steamships with passenger accommodation aboard, it was limited, and expensive.

The accommodation on most ships was basic. The passenger facilities were also lacking. The saloon would double as both dining venue and after-dinner lounge. On-deck areas were largely taken up by working spaces and were also shared with livestock that was carried aboard for the purposes of supplying food for the passengers and crew.

Bathing and toileting facilities were limited, with passengers sharing bathrooms, although having a bath aboard was not a guarantee. Some ships had none, while others had one that had to be shared between all passengers and was filled with salt water. Lighting on board was provided by lamps and candles, which added an increased risk of fire on board.

Steamships in the early years were fitted with masts and sails and would operate under sail power when the winds were favourable. The sails could also be used to try to stabilise the vessel somewhat, which was especially important on ships that were fitted with paddle wheels as these were only effective when in the water, and when the seas were rough, one or the other wheel would often lift out of the water entirely, rendering it ineffective.

The ships were small by today's standards and often faced rough weather. Crew and passengers would at times need to tie themselves onto some part of the ship in order to avoid being washed overboard or thrown out of bed in the evening. Still, despite these discomforts, they were an upgrade on the sailing ships, being able to provide a much more reliable service, with a reasonable guarantee of getting to one's destination on time.

The ability of steamships to effectively operate on a regular schedule was of great importance for those sending cargo as well. One of the most lucrative types of cargo was the mails. But this also came with strict conditions regarding the timeliness of the service.

Government mail contracts were sought after because they provided a set fee for shipping lines to carry mails on their ships. These contracts provided regular income, which allowed the shipping companies to build bigger and faster ships. The regular income also allowed the shipping companies to introduce new services and new destinations.

For example, PSN Co. in 1840 submitted a tender for a British government mail contract to carry mails from London to Alexandria. Being contracted for this service allowed them to expand their reach much further east than their original Iberian Peninsula itineraries. Following their successful tender, the company was incorporated by Royal Charter, becoming the Peninsular & Oriental Steam Navigation Company (P&O) to reflect their expansion plans.

Brunel's engineering prowess was highlighted once again in 1843, with the design and construction of a large iron-hulled liner named *Great Britain*. Developed for the Great Western Steam Navigation Co., the ship clocked in at 3,675 tons and spanned over 98m (321ft) from stem to stern. These dimensions were impressive for the time, with the vessel being the largest steamship yet built.

Great Britain was a ship that changed the course of marine engineering, but her construction also had a significant impact worldwide. *Great Britain* was originally designed to be the largest paddle steamer ever.

The scale of the ship required a significant propulsion system, of a size not yet seen at sea. Francis Humphries was selected as the engine builder. The size of the paddle shaft required for *Great Britain* was so great that it was unable to be forged with the existing technology.

Humphries wrote to his friend and engineer, James Nasmyth saying, 'I find, there is not a forge-hammer in England or Scotland powerful enough to forge the paddle-shaft of the engine for the *Great Britain*! What am I to do?'

Nasmyth's response was to draft the first steam hammer design. However, before Nasmyth's hammer became a reality, Brunel opted to utilise the screw propeller for the *Great Britain*, negating the need for paddle wheels and thus the extremely large paddle shaft.

Ultimately, other engineers were the first to build the steam hammer, but Nasmyth was still able to patent his own design in 1843. He would later go on to adapt and refine the steam hammer design, which became very popular around the country.

The adoption of the propeller for *Great Britain* was a milestone in the development of that technology. *Great Britain*'s design was already under way when the first ocean-going steamship to successfully employ the screw propeller entered service.

Owned by the Ship Propeller Company, the wooden-hulled *Archimedes* of 1839 utilised a screw propeller design created by Francis Smith, one of the pioneers of propeller technology.

Archimedes successfully proved the technology could be utilised on a steamer of 237 tons. While early propellers were used to move water in ancient China, the first incarnation of propeller technology on a ship took place aboard the *Civetta*. Designed by Austrian–Czech inventor Joseph Russell, the screw-propelled vessel achieved a top speed of 6 knots before development work halted.

Independently, Nova Scotian John Patch developed a hand-cranked, double-bladed propeller for his fishing boats. With the design showing promise, Patch scaled up his invention for use aboard the 25-ton schooner *Royal George*.

As with many innovations, there were multiple approaches taken, and it was ultimately engineers John Ericsson and Francis Smith that were the most lauded. Ericsson is remembered for his work with the United States Navy, with his propeller design being employed aboard the USS *Princeton*. Smith built the *Archimedes* using his own propeller patent.

With a viable alternative propulsion technology came numerous competitions between paddle wheel and screw propeller vessels, aimed at proving which was the best. One of the most famous was the competition between the naval vessels HMS *Rattler* and HMS *Alecto*, which took place in 1845. It culminated in a tug of war, where the ships, attached to each other at the stern by a hawser, both steamed at full power in opposite directions. *Rattler*, the propeller-driven ship, was able to tow *Alecto* backwards at 2.8 knots.

The example of *Archimedes* prompted Brunel to switch *Great Britain*'s propulsion from the originally proposed paddle wheels to a propeller. Likewise, the example of the *Rainbow*, the largest iron-hulled steamer in service in 1838, was said to be a deciding factor in Brunel's decision to build *Great Britain* with an iron hull as well.

Great Britain was an important ship in that she brought together a number of different innovations and showed others what could be done. Though it took some years before these innovations would be adopted more widely, this ship opened the door to future designs.

While *Great Britain* was not a commercial success, the Cunard Line service was proving to be both profitable and popular. Within the first five years of operation they were able to build two new, larger ships, *Cambria* and *Hibernia*, with a further four ships entering service in 1848.

Great Britain (1845–86). *Great Britain* was raised in 1970 and returned to the dry dock where it was built. Today the ship is operated as a museum ship and is open to the public. (Frame & Cross)

HMS *Warrior* (1860–83). Steamships were powered by coal, which had to be hand shovelled into the boilers. Boiler rooms were located low in the ship and stokers suffered from heat, coal dust and poor ventilation. (Frame & Cross)

Great Britain (1845–86). *Great Britain* is fitted with replica passenger accommodation, which gives an idea of what it would have been like to travel aboard the ship during her years as a liner. (Frame & Cross)

Far left: *Great Britain* (1845–86). *Great Britain* was fitted with a screw propeller. *Great Britain*'s propeller was direct drive, with the steam engine attached directly to the propeller. (Frame & Cross)

Left: *Great Britain* (1845–86). Steering aboard the early ocean liners was largely accomplished using a rudder. This could be adjusted from the bridge and the engine room, to change the ship's course. (Frame & Cross)

DID YOU KNOW?

There is a crater on the moon named after James Nasmyth, who had an interest in astronomy.

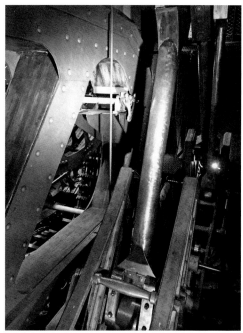

Great Britain (1845–86). When *Great Britain* first entered service it carried passengers in a single class. Though very different to what we expect today, the dining room was well appointed for its time. (Frame & Cross)

Great Britain (1845–86). *Great Britain* had a 1,000hp steam engine, the most powerful used at sea at the time. (Frame & Cross)

Great Britain (1845–86). The ship's bell was used to indicate time aboard and to signal its location during fog. The name of the ship is usually engraved on the bell. (Frame & Cross)

America, *Canada*, *Europa* and *Niagara* were all larger in size and faster than their predecessors and capable of carrying 140 passengers each. They were notable as being the first ships to use coloured signal lights at night to aid with navigation. The use of red for port and green for starboard was standardised across shipping (and later aviation) and is still used to this day.

The New York and Liverpool United States Mail Steamship Company was founded in 1848 and was known popularly as the Collins Line. Under the direction of Edward Knight Collins, the company bid for and was awarded the United States Postmaster General's subsidised mail service. This allowed them to build a fleet of four ships to operate a transatlantic mail and passenger service.

Collins Line was determined to build ships that were better in all ways than the Cunard liners, seeing them as their greatest competition. The Collins Line ships were bigger, faster and provided superior passenger amenities. When their first ship, *Atlantic*, entered service in 1850 it featured running water, ventilation in all passenger accommodation areas, and even a steam heating system to keep passengers warm on the chilly Atlantic. The ship also had a bathing cabin and a hairdressing salon.

The speed of the Collins Line ships made them popular with passengers, and their ships *Pacific*, *Baltic* and *Arctic* undertook record-breaking crossings of the Atlantic. But this came at a price. Running the ships at such high speeds significantly increased their coal consumption and also led to high repair costs, as the wooden-hulled ships were not strong enough to withstand such high speeds without regular, expensive maintenance.

In 1850 the Liverpool and Philadelphia Steamship Company was formed. Better known as the Inman Line, they purchased the *City of Glasgow* from her builder, Tod & Macgregor. *City of Glasgow* was an iron-hulled screw steamer. Taking almost four days longer to cross the Atlantic than the fastest ship of the day, Cunard's *Asia*, *City of Glasgow* was not built for speed. What she was, was economical.

Running the ship at a slower speed meant a significant saving in coal; more than 50 tons per day. Having an iron hull also led to cost savings, as iron-hulled steamers were stronger and required less maintenance and repairs, as well as not being prone to woodworm or rot.

The *City of Glasgow* was significant in her ability to be operated profitably, without a government contract. Not having a fixed income may have helped the Inman Line to innovate. In 1852 the line refitted *City of Glasgow* to install dedicated steerage accommodation. Having specific accommodation for steerage passengers, separate from livestock and cargo, and including a separate place for passengers to eat, was a vast improvement on what had come before.

Steerage accommodation, prior to this, had mostly involved the poorest passengers being crammed into whatever spaces were left below decks. Lack of toileting facilities and ventilation, together with overcrowding, led to disease running wild in these spaces. Not all passengers survived the journey.

Though cheaper than travelling first or second class, steerage could still be an expensive proposition for those with little funds, trying to emigrate to find a better life. The Inman Line prices were higher than many of their competitors. Inman Line did offer several benefits over many other lines of the time, including providing better ventilation and allowing steerage passengers to access the ship's surgeon. Those travelling steerage class aboard their ships were also given two hot meals per day.

Incredibly, in the early years shipping companies did not provide food for all passengers on board. While first class and second class generally had food included in their fare, those travelling steerage class often had to bring their own for the crossing. In a time when ships could be delayed significantly by weather conditions and other ill luck, this occasionally led to disastrous outcomes for the poorest passengers. Though regulations surrounding the feeding of passengers were introduced in 1819 and again in the 1850s, these were often treated more like guidelines.

Though sailing ships were still being operated on many routes and would be for many years to come, they were no longer the premium way to travel. The newspapers were now littered with mentions of the newest, fastest and most luxurious steamships. Passengers flocked to the better-known ships, further boosting their profits. The Atlantic liners were held to be of high prestige, and the details of the new ships being launched often made headlines as far away as Australia.

New innovations aboard ships caught the public's attention. With each successive ship to improve the speed record, or improve the on-board experience in some material way, the shipping lines grew in reputation. As did the pride of the nation to which the line belonged.

In 1854 the keel of Brunel's final steamship was laid down. The path to building this ship had not been an easy one. Brunel had been thinking of building a new vessel since the World Exhibition in 1851. His new ship was to be larger than any that had come before her. Brunel was certain that a ship of large dimensions, he suggested 600ft × 65ft × 30ft (182.8m × 19.8m × 9.1m), would benefit from economies of scale.

The new ship was to have both a screw propeller and paddle wheels as well as auxiliary sails. He approached shipbuilder John Scott Russell. Russell made the calculations and determined that despite the monumental size that Brunel had suggested, it was possible to build such a ship. The vessel would require engines capable of producing 8,500hp in order to reach speeds of 14 knots.

This ship was to be built for the Eastern Steam Navigation Company, which initially wanted to use it for the emigrant trade from Britain to Australia. But, in order for the ship to be commercially viable on this route, it required a government mail contract. Though they tendered for the contract, it was awarded to P&O.

Brunel had originally envisioned this massive ship as a transatlantic liner, and with the failure to secure a mail contract on the Australian route, the Eastern Steam Navigation Company turned its interest in this direction.

The new ship was launched in January 1858. She had been christened *Leviathan*, but later became known as *Great Eastern*. And, like Brunel's earlier two ships, she was revolutionary in design.

Great Eastern was iron hulled and the hull contained both longitudinal and transverse bulkheads, dividing it into watertight compartments. She was also the first ship to incorporate a double hull. This offered greater safety to those aboard should the ship ever suffer a collision at sea.

Despite her size, stability and safety aspects, *Great Eastern* was not a successful transatlantic liner. The Eastern Steam Navigation Company entered liquidation during the ship's fitting out and *Great Eastern* was then acquired by the Great Steam Navigation Company. The maiden voyage was disrupted when a large explosion aboard caused the deaths of several crew members and severe damage to the ship. Brunel died on 15 September 1859, but his legacy lived on. It would be decades before another ship would match the size of *Great Eastern*.

Though a failure as a transatlantic passenger liner, *Great Eastern* did make a significant contribution to international communications when she was chartered in 1865 to lay the second transatlantic telephone cable.

The first undersea cable had been run between England and France. Laying a cable across the Atlantic was another matter entirely. The first undersea cable across the Atlantic required multiple attempts before it was successfully laid in 1858. The cable failed three weeks after completion. Nonetheless, the initial success of the cable proved that such a feat was possible.

Great Eastern's first attempt at laying the second transatlantic cable in 1865 was also unsuccessful. The cable snapped before it reached its destination, and the attempt was abandoned. The following year a cable was successfully laid using the *Great Eastern*, and after that success they returned to the point where the cable had snapped the previous year and managed to reconnect it and complete that line, too.

The laying of undersea cables was a milestone for communications. Where once there was no option but to send messages by post across the ocean, now there was the option to send them by telegraph. The possibilities this opened up for business were immense.

Also in 1866, Inman Line's *City of Paris* became the first screw-driven ship to match the operational speed of the paddle wheel ships. This proved to be a turning point for the design of new vessels. Screw propellers had long proved the potential to be the more economical method of propelling a ship. Now that they could also move a ship at speed, the screw propeller began to supplant the paddle wheel as the more popular form of propulsion.

Though propellers had proven early on to be efficient and therefore economical to run, there had been serious issues to overcome before they could be comfortably employed on passenger ships. The two main issues were vibrations, caused by the operation of the propeller, and cavitation, caused by the way the propeller interacted with the water around it.

As a propeller spins it creates differences in pressure. This causes nearby water to move in to fill a negative pressure void, allowing the propeller to create forward motion in the process. But this movement also causes vibrations as the pressure generated by the motion of the propeller interacts with the underside of the hull.

Opposite page. Clockwise from top: *City of Paris* (1889–1923). The second Inman Line ship to bear the name *City of Paris*, this ship held the Blue Riband from 1889 to 1891 and again from 1892 to 1893. (Michael W. Pocock/www.maritimequest.com); *Great Eastern* (1858–89). The largest ship then put to sea, *Great Eastern* was initially named *Leviathan*. It was sold due to the owners' financial difficulties and renamed *Great Eastern*. (Michael W. Pocock/www.maritimequest.com); *Great Eastern* (1858–89). *Great Eastern* was constructed by John Scott Russell & Co. The ship was so large that the first attempt to launch it in November 1857 failed. It was finally launched in January 1858. (Michael W. Pocock/www.maritimequest.com)

Right: *Great Eastern* (1858–89). After being used to lay transatlantic telegraph cables, *Great Eastern* was used as a floating dance hall and then as a floating billboard for the department store Lewis's. (Michael W. Pocock/www.maritimequest.com)

DID YOU KNOW?

Great Britain remained in use for decades in different roles and configurations. She was in service as a steamship, steam clipper and sailing ship, transporting passengers, immigrants and cargo, before becoming a storage bunker. At the end of her life she was scuttled in the Falkland Islands. In 1970 the ship was raised and towed back to Britain, where she remains as a museum ship in the dry dock where she was built.

In extreme cases, most noticeable when the propeller rotation is high, the areas of low pressure on the propeller blade become so low that it creates vapour build-up around the blade. When this happens, the vapour is carried with the blade until it meets an area of higher pressure. This causes the vapour bubbles to implode in a process known as cavitation. The effect is further discomfort, particularly at the aft of the ship, as well as reduced efficiency and, in worst cases, damage to the propeller blades due to the impact of the implosions.

There had been many experiments to try and overcome these issues, with inventors trialling different propeller shapes, numbers of blades and revolutions. Although there had been many improvements by the time *City of Paris* came into service, the problem had not been fully solved, and still arises with modern ships.

Using screw propellers and their associated machinery to propel a ship fundamentally changed the layout of the midships area aboard. By necessity, on a paddle steamer much of the drive machinery was situated amidships in a vertical arrangement. This meant that the passenger and cargo areas were mostly clustered towards the bow and stern.

A ship fitted with a propeller had its machinery arranged differently, with the machinery located further aft and lower within the hull.

Removing the paddle wheels opened up the midships area for passenger facilities and additional cargo space. This allowed ships to increase passenger capacity and also introduce new passenger amenities.

THE CRUISE HOLIDAY

Today we are well acquainted with the idea of a cruise holiday. You board the ship, unpack your luggage and enjoy an itinerary designed specifically for the pleasure voyage. But early 'cruise' holidays were not run in the same way as modern ones.

In the 1840s, P&O offered pleasure voyages known as the 'Grand Tour'. One such P&O sailing from 1843 lists ports of call in Gibraltar, Malta, Athens, Syria, Smyrna, Mytilene, the Dardanelles and Constantinople undertaken aboard the 909-ton steamer *Tagus*. It was advertised under the headline of 'Interesting and Classic Excursion'.

The following year, P&O invited the author William Thackeray on a Grand Tour, in a move that resembles the modern cruise ship media familiarisation. Cruising for pleasure was so new, and the chance of problems arising so great, that it could easily have backfired on P&O.

However, Thackeray went on to write a detailed account of his experience aboard the various P&O ships used to undertake a Mediterranean tour. His works were published in 1845 under the title *Notes from a journey from Cornhill to Cairo, by way of Lisbon, Athens, Constantinople and Jerusalem*, often shortened by readers to *From Cornhill to Cairo, Etc.* The subtitle of the book was *Performed in the Steamers of the Peninsular and Oriental Company*, which was boldly embossed on the cover.

Thackeray's work illustrated an interesting peculiarity of early cruising: the voyage was often undertaken on multiple vessels. These ships were for all intents and purposes ocean liners, undertaking scheduled line voyages. P&O's genius was to package the various voyages up into a single experience, marketed to those brave, and wealthy enough, to attempt it.

American writer Mark Twain did in America what Thackeray had done in the United Kingdom, popularising the notion of a pleasure voyage. In the late 1860s, Twain undertook a voyage aboard the 1,451-ton steamer *Quaker City*, calling at several Mediterranean ports.

He published his experience in the novel *The Innocents Abroad*, which chronicles amusing and adventurous anecdotes from his five-month journey. The book was an instant hit, becoming a bestseller and catapulting the concept of a cruise voyage into popular culture, even though only the wealthy could afford to undertake such a journey.

4

CHANGING THE SHAPE OF THE WORLD

In 1869 the Suez Canal was opened, creating a direct sea passage between the Red Sea and the Mediterranean. This opened up new possibilities for passenger and cargo transportation, as well as decreasing the transit time and connections required for movement from European ports to Asian, Australian and New Zealand destinations.

But the Suez Canal had many teething issues, and despite the convenience that it offered, it wasn't an easy transition for some shipping companies.

P&O was one of the biggest shipping companies operating between Britain and India and Australia at the time. They had built their services to India and onward to Australia using two separate fleets of ships. One fleet was based between Britain and Alexandria, in the Mediterranean. The other was based between Suez and the many ports they serviced in India and onwards.

Their biggest competitor was Compagnie des Services Maritimes Imperiales, which operated a number of routes, including between Marseilles and Alexandria. They also ran ships between Suez and French Indochina (now Vietnam), with feeder services to Saigon, Hong Kong, Shanghai and Yokohama.

Both shipping lines had built infrastructure around the pre-Suez Canal operating environment. P&O for example, in addition to investing heavily in coaling stations, dockyards, repair facilities and warehouses along their route, had also invested in overland passenger routes, barges and tugs for the Mahmoudieh Canal, steamers on the Nile and a hotel and farm in Cairo.

With the opening of the Suez Canal, these assets became largely obsolete. No longer did passengers and cargo need to disembark in Alexandria before travelling overland to meet another ship in the Red Sea. Now the ship that left Britain could be the one to arrive in Australia.

Furthermore, for P&O at least, they were still contractually obliged to stop in Alexandria and put off the mails, to be carried by the overland route. The alternative to this was to accept a significant reduction in their government mail contract, which would have further damaged the line's finances.

The established lines were now faced with a problem. The Suez Canal opening had meant a significant write down in the value of their assets. They also needed new ships, for the new operating environment. And the number of competitors had increased substantially, further challenging their supremacy.

In fact, competition was increasing around the world as new shipping lines started up, taking advantage of the rapidly evolving technology for driving ships. Compound engines were becoming more popular, with many established shipping lines, including P&O, choosing to upgrade their existing fleet.

On the Atlantic the Oceanic Steam Navigation Company's White Star Line commenced operations in 1871 with their purpose-built ship *Oceanic*. Built by Harland & Wolff in Belfast, *Oceanic* was a single-screw ship with compound engines. Her iron hull was completed with eleven watertight compartments.

Oceanic had a maximum capacity of 166 first-class passengers and 1,000 more in steerage. Her first-class accommodation was located amidships, taking advantage of the stability of that part of the ship, and keeping it away from the engine vibrations. The first-class dining room was large enough to accommodate all of the first-class passengers in one seating.

Oceanic had a number of other innovations, including having a separate berth or bed for each passenger in steerage class. This was a huge improvement for these people, who had previously been required to share sleeping space with other passengers. Steerage travellers were segregated, with single men berthed at the forward end of the ship and families, married couples and single women berthed in the stern.

Visually, *Oceanic* was different, with a superstructure that combined what had previously been multiple deckhouses into a consolidated structure that extended the full width of the ship. This design was able to offer more indoor space for passenger amenities and a small number of passenger cabins.

Over the next two years White Star Line put several more ships into service, with their new builds being of the same high standard set by *Oceanic*. This included *Oceanic*'s sister ships, *Atlantic*, *Baltic* and *Republic*, two smaller ships purchased and trialled on the Suez route, the *Tropic* and *Asiatic*, and two larger Atlantic liners, *Adriatic* and *Celtic*.

In May 1872 *Adriatic* took the westbound Atlantic speed record, completing the crossing in seven days, twenty-three hours and seventeen minutes. White Star Line could now boast both the fastest and the most comfortable transatlantic crossing. They were also developing a reputation for safety at sea.

Another successful line was founded in 1871 as Plate, Reuchlin & Co. They commenced services in 1872 between Rotterdam and New York with their ship *Rotterdam*, a 1,694-ton steamer. *Rotterdam* was followed by another ship, *Maas*, and the two were engaged in a monthly service. In 1873 the company was reorganised with a new partner and became Nederlandsch-Amerikaansche Stoomvaart Maatschappij (NASM, later known as Holland-America Line).

The NASM ships were smaller than many other contemporary transatlantic liners, as their vessels needed to fit into the locks at Hellevoetsluis. The shipping line also faced early difficulties with the Panic of 1873.

The economic downturn in both Europe and the United States began in September 1873 and lasted until 1879 in parts of Europe. The downturn in passengers and cargo put many shipping companies under financial strain.

DID YOU KNOW?

'Steerage' is so called because the accommodation for these passengers was originally in the same areas of the ship as the steering gears.

Clockwise from top left: *Orient* (1879–1910). When the Suez Canal was first opened it was only wide enough for one-way traffic. Ships would stop in passing bays to allow the oncoming traffic to pass before continuing on their journey. (Henderson & Cremer Collection); White Star Line house flag. White Star Line commenced transatlantic operations in 1871 when the Oceanic Steam Navigation Company purchased the house flag and goodwill of the defunct packet company, White Star Line. (Frame & Cross); *Austral* (1882–1903). Shipping was not without risk, especially in the early days. Orient Line's *Austral* sank in Sydney Harbour in 1882 whilst re-coaling. It took several months before the ship could be raised. Not every ship was so lucky. (Henderson & Cremer Collection)

City of Berlin (1875–1921). Inman Line's *City of Berlin* won the Blue Riband in 1875. She was transferred to American Line in 1893 when Inman Line was purchased by IMM Co. (Michael W. Pocock/www.maritimequest.com)

Orient (1879–1910). The busy waterway of the Suez Canal revolutionised transportation between Europe and Asia. However, at first, the canal was quite narrow, as witnessed here with *Orient* tied up to make way for a passing ship. (Henderson & Cremer Collection)

Orient (1879–1910). *Orient* under way, showing off her four masts, twin funnels and built-up white superstructure. (Henderson & Cremer Collection)

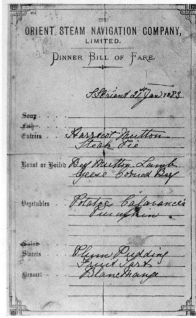

MENU CARD — ORIENT, 1883

Opposite page: Clockwise from top left:
Orient (1879–1910). Docked in Sydney Harbour, *Orient* shares the waterway with sailing vessels and small boats while onlookers catch a glimpse from the banks. (Henderson & Cremer Collection); Dinner menu *Orient* (21 January 1883). Dinner aboard ships in the 1880s was largely made up of meat and starchy vegetables and was greatly improved from the earliest steamship menus that relied wholly on preserves and other items that would keep well during long stretches at sea. (Henderson & Cremer Collection); *Ceylon* (1858–82). *Ceylon* was a three-masted steamship built for P&O. In 1882 the ship attempted a world cruise for her new owners the Inter-Oceanic Yachting Company Limited. (Henderson & Cremer Collection)

In addition to the financial conditions, not every route was profitable for every shipping line. White Star Line's forays into the Liverpool to Calcutta via Suez route were unprofitable, and they instead moved *Tropic* and *Asiatic* onto the Liverpool to Valparaiso route. This too proved unsuccessful. But it was far from the only problem White Star was facing.

In 1873, during a westbound Atlantic crossing, *Atlantic* struck rocks off the coast of Halifax. A total of 585 people died in the disaster and the ship was lost. This led to a crisis of confidence from the travelling public and *Tropic* and *Asiatic* were sold to cover the line's financial losses.

Despite the ongoing depression both White Star Line and Cunard Line built bigger and faster ships for the Atlantic trade during 1874. That same year F. Green & Co. and Anderson, Anderson & Co., two shipping lines that had previously operated sailing ships to the Australian Colonies, partnered to offer two steamship sailings. One ran from London to Sydney and the other from London to Melbourne. The voyages were successful and would lead to the foundation of the Orient Steam Navigation Company Limited.

It was not just the proliferation of new shipping lines that was making changes on the waves. There were also a number of new technological innovations that were about to change the face of shipping forever.

Despite a number of early failures, in 1877 two French cargo ships, *Le Frigorifique* and *Paraguay*, made successful Atlantic crossings carrying cargo that included refrigerated meat. This was a huge step forward in terms of allowing international trade of refrigerated goods, but it also had effects on passenger shipping.

Until the advent of refrigeration on ships, food and provisions for those on board was often preserved. Early ships carried livestock aboard, such as chickens for eggs and meat, pigs and even a cow for milk. With the introduction of refrigeration for provisions, suddenly a whole world of new culinary options opened up. The ability to carry fresh fruit, vegetables and meat that would stay fresh throughout the journey was a great improvement.

Other technological marvels were making their way onto ships as well. In 1879, Inman Line's *City of Berlin* became the first transatlantic liner fitted with electric lighting.

Up until this time, ships had mostly been lit by paraffin lamps or candles. White Star Line's *Adriatic* trialled a system using gas lighting aboard, but it proved unsuccessful. Though the naysayers believed electric lighting aboard a ship to be a disaster waiting to happen, it was a vast improvement on the dim and uncertain illumination that had come before. But it would take years before electric lighting was rolled out across all ships.

In 1882, there was a development of a different kind when the British steamer *Ceylon* departed from Southampton on a bold and adventurous world cruise. With a gross registered tonnage (grt) of 2,110, the ship was built for P&O in 1858 by the Samunda Brothers at their Poplar yard on the Thames.

The ship was sold by P&O to the Inter-Oceanic Yachting Co. Ltd in 1881, with the new owners planning to sail the ship around the world. Articles in the *Daily News* from 1881 hint at the forthcoming voyage, noting, 'every accommodation has been made for conveying private servants of passengers and the vessel is so arranged that the latter will have the whole of the main deck to themselves'.

While the voyage was notable as the first attempt to 'cruise' around the world, only forty passengers opted to join the ship, leaving sixty of the 100 berths empty. As a result, it was deemed a financial failure and was not repeated.

Routes between Europe, the Far East, Australia and New Zealand were also becoming easier due to improvements in the Suez Canal. When the canal first opened it was very narrow, limiting both the size and number of vessels that could transit the waterway. Over the years following its opening the canal was widened, but the passage was very congested, which led to long delays.

In 1886 P&O's ship *Carthage* became the first ship to transit the Suez Canal at night. Night transits had a major effect in reducing congestion in the canal.

The 1880s saw new shipping lines start up. Canadian Pacific Line commenced transpacific services in 1887 using chartered ships. The line was an offshoot of the Canadian Pacific Railway Co., and their early services were marketed under the Railway brand. They won a mail contract to transport mails from Britain to Hong Kong via Canada in 1891, and for this service built three ships to operate the transpacific portion of the route. These ships, the *Empress of India*, *Empress of China* and *Empress of Japan*, were twin-screw vessels of 5,905 grt each.

HURRICANE DECK OF THE P. & O. CO'S S.S. CARTHAGE: LOOKING AFT.

SALOON OF THE P. & O. CO'S S.S. CARTHAGE.

Carthage (1881–1903). A view along the Hurricane Deck of the *Carthage* shows a very different arrangement to modern passenger ships. An open bridge is positioned ahead of twin smokestacks as well as masts that can be fully rigged. (Henderson & Cremer Collection)

Carthage (1881–1903). This interior view of P&O's *Carthage* shows the main saloon of the liner. Large banquet tables sit between swivel seating that is bolted to the floor, to stop the chairs from moving in rough seas. After dinner, these chairs could be swivelled outwards, allowing passengers to converse with one another. (Henderson & Cremer Collection)

Chimborazo (1871–97). Originally chartered from PSN. Co., *Chimborazo* was purchased by Orient Line in 1878. The ship was one of the early cruising pioneers. (Henderson & Cremer Collection)

Garonne (1871–1905). *Garonne* was a single-screw liner powered by a coal-fired, two-cylinder compound engine. The ship was used on the Australian run before becoming a full-time cruise ship in 1889. She was broken up in 1905. (Henderson & Cremer Collection)

Garonne at Station de Kantaru. The Suez Canal passage in the nineteenth century was quite different from a modern transit of the waterway. Steamships could call at stations along the way to take on provisions and mails. (Henderson & Cremer Collection)

Orient (1879–1910). *Orient* was rebuilt in 1898, completely changing her exterior appearance. Her twin funnels were replaced by a single, taller stack, while two of her masts were removed. (Henderson & Cremer Collection)

The first twin-screw ship had been put to sea in 1863. Twin-screw, and later, triple- and quadruple-screw, ships solved many of the problems that had plagued those with only a single propeller.

Single-screw ships were vulnerable to a number of issues due to a lack of redundancy. If that propeller, the propeller shaft or associated machinery were damaged or lost during a voyage then the ship was left unable to use its steam engines. It was nearly impossible to repair or replace a propeller at sea, and the chances of repairing or replacing the shaft were similarly remote. In these cases, ships would have to be rigged for sail, or be towed to port by another vessel.

With the introduction of twin propellers, a ship would still be able to continue to make way under steam even if one of its propellers was damaged or lost. This eventually allowed shipping lines to do away with the need for auxiliary sails. Though the main mast and the foremast remained for various other purposes, they were no longer able to be rigged for sail.

It wasn't just ships undertaking line voyages that were changing. The North of Scotland & Orkney & Shetland Steam Navigation Company (the North Company) had traditionally operated a fleet of coastal steamers in the waters around Britain. In 1887 their newest ship, St Sunniva, entered service.

A very small ship by today's standards, St Sunniva was only 71.9m (236ft) long and 960 grt. She had accommodation for up to 142 passengers in a single class. Where she differed from her contemporaries was that St Sunniva was a purpose-built cruise ship.

The ship was built by Hall Russell & Co. Ltd in Aberdeen and was constructed with triple-expansion steam reciprocating engines. It was capable of achieving 15.5 knots. As it was built as a cruise vessel, the ship had no cargo storage areas. Instead, the space was devoted to passenger accommodation and facilities. The rooms were shared, with shared toilet facilities.

The experience on board was very different to what we expect from a cruise holiday today. Entertainment was limited to what could be provided by the passengers. There was a piano for use by the guests, and on some voyages the passengers wrote their own newspaper.

The North Company operated cruise itineraries to the Norwegian fjords, Baltic cruises and round Britain cruises with St Sunniva, as well as utilising their coastal steamer St Rognvald for cruising during the summer. For several years they faced very little competition. St Sunniva in particular attracted crowds of inquisitive onlookers in many of her ports, with the general public keen to capture a glimpse of a ship carrying passengers for fun.

The North Company's solitary fulltime cruising foray was short-lived. St Sunniva and St Rognvald had proved the viability of the concept, so it wasn't long before other companies entered the market with ships of their own.

In 1889 Orient Line became one of the first major competitors that the North Company faced, when they put their Australian steamers Chimborazo and Garonne into the cruise market. Chimborazo, at 3,847 grt and 117m (384ft) long, and Garonne, at 3,876 grt and 116.5m (382ft) long, were significantly bigger than either of the North Company cruise ships. The Orient Line vessels also boasted superior passenger accommodations and facilities.

Chimborazo and Garonne proved so successful in their cruising roles that they were withdrawn from the Australian mail service that same year and commenced a regular cruising schedule from London for the Orient Line.

In 1891 Hamburg-Amerika Line commenced cruising with the 7,661-grt Auguste Victoria. The fifty-eight-day cruise called at fourteen ports, with 241 passengers joining the ship for the excursion.

Most notable was the fact that Auguste Victoria was the largest German liner at the time, adding to the public intrigue that surrounded the sailing. German painter Christian Wilhelm Allers joined the cruise and wrote the on-board newspaper.

Hamburg-Amerika pushed the cruising envelope again at the turn of the twentieth century when it introduced the 4,409-grt Prinzessin Victoria Luise. This elegant vessel was painted completely in white, sporting twin funnels. A bowsprit and twin masts gave the impression of a luxurious yacht, yet the ship was built specifically for year-round cruising.

Her interior spaces featured extravagant finishes, with the vessel containing staterooms exclusively for first-class passengers. Her cruise itineraries took in Mediterranean, Baltic and Caribbean ports, with tours organised for passengers when going ashore.

EARLY CRUISING PIONEER

While not a cruise ship owner, Thomas Cook saw an opportunity to organise cruise holidays aboard existing steamers. With a wide-reaching network, Thomas Cook was able to negotiate bulk rates and offered (relatively) affordable convenient access to escorted holidays, in a style akin to a modern, upscale travel agency.

Thomas Cook's foray into this market started in the 1870s, with the organisation offering an escorted round the world tour. This trip included a variety of transportation methods, from ferries and railways to transatlantic and transpacific steamship crossings.

Buoyed by the success, the organisation started to expand its offering, with the first Thomas Cook-sponsored cruises to the North Sea, West Indies and the Middle East all setting sail in the 1880s.

5

BUILDING FOR PURPOSE

Cruising appealed to shipping lines, as it gave voyage planners the opportunity to find alternative uses for their ships, especially in the leaner months where line voyages saw less commerce and trade. But it would be a long time before cruising would take over as the dominant passenger shipping market.

In the meantime, most passenger shipping companies relied on a very similar base concept, some combination of passenger and cargo transportation across a specific route or routes. But the ships they employed became increasingly different in design as time went on.

These differences were influenced by many factors, including the conditions they were to operate in, the money the company had to play with, passenger preferences and even the personal preferences of the owners and managing directors. Samuel Cunard, for example, preferred paddle wheels to propellers and Cunard's express ships were built with paddle wheels until 1862. *Scotia*, which was the last Cunard express liner built with paddle wheels, was also the last paddle wheel ship to hold the speed record for a transatlantic crossing.

While cruise ships generally had shorter distances to cover, and thus had looser expectations around speed of the vessel, the mail ships did not. They were required to maintain a certain speed for their service in order to meet the stipulations of their contracts. Lines that could provide faster cargo and passenger crossings could also attract higher fares and increased trade.

The transit between Europe and the Americas was held to be a route of some prestige. Passengers on these voyages, both first class and steerage, had certain expectations from the ships they travelled on, and in addition to speed requirements, passenger demands also helped to shape the ships that plied these routes.

The early liners had set the expectation for the hull of the ship to be painted in dark colours above the waterline. The dark colours helped hide the coal dust that would inevitably accumulate on the sides of the hull during refuelling. Additionally, the dark hull would retain heat in cooler climates.

While the dark hull colour made sense on a lot of northern hemisphere routes, it had downsides for ships built to transit the tropics. Some of the early cruise ships, such as *Prinzessin Victoria Luise*, were painted with a white hull. The Canadian Pacific *Empress* liners were also painted with light-coloured hulls. This would have helped keep the ships cooler when they were sailing in warmer weather.

Regardless of the hull colour above the waterline, the ship was generally a different colour from the waterline down. The old wooden-hulled ships were often fitted with thin sheets of copper or copper alloy below the waterline, which was an early anti-fouling measure.

Anti-fouling materials are used to prevent the growth and build-up of marine life on the underside of a ship, which would impact its speed and performance, as well as its longevity.

In wooden-hulled ships, shipworms were a real threat to the integrity of the hull, while on all ships, barnacles and other marine growths cause drag in the water, which slows their speed and makes them more inefficient to run.

From the 1860s onwards, as more and more ships began to be built of iron and later steel, the copper sheeting was replaced with anti-fouling paint. This was red due to the cuprous oxide it contained.

The anti-fouling solutions worked by poisoning any organism nearby, as the copper leached into the water around the ship. This prevented animals and marine growth from attaching to the hull and slowing the vessel down.

As ships grew in size, the superstructure became larger and a bigger feature of the ship. White Star Line's *Oceanic* of 1871 is often credited with changing the shape of the passenger ship above the hull. *Oceanic* combined the separate deckhouses into one, creating the superstructure.

The Norddeutscher Lloyd liner *Elbe*, which entered service in 1881, introduced an additional deck to her superstructure, allowing for larger passenger spaces. Over time many other ships copied these changes, with superstructures becoming bigger, with increased numbers of decks above the hull. The superstructure was often painted in a lighter colour, such as white, which contrasted with the darker hull.

The aesthetic differences between the superstructures of the various ships were not just limited to colour. As the superstructure of ships grew in size throughout the late nineteenth and early twentieth century, the differences in design became more apparent.

Ships built for colder climates benefitted from more enclosed spaces. Some vessels featured enclosed promenades, allowing passengers, especially those in first class, to stroll the deck while sheltered from the elements.

But it wasn't practical, or comfortable, for ships travelling through warmer climates to be the same as those ships built for the cold. On summer passages that crossed the equator, passengers suffered greatly from the heat, with many instances of illness and death caused by the soaring temperatures.

As a result, those ships built for lines such as P&O and Orient often had much more open superstructures. This allowed for more outdoor spaces, with shade from higher decks and often canvas sails stretched across the uppermost decks. As ventilation in below decks areas aboard ships was often limited, and journeys were often of long duration, the ability to get out on deck and get some fresh air, even if it was hot outside, was extremely important.

At the top of the ship the funnels were painted in the house colours of the shipping line to which they belonged. This helped observers to identify the ship, and its line, over distance. The tops of these funnels were often black, whether by design, or simply because the soot coming from the funnels left them this colour.

For example, the White Star liners had buff-coloured funnels, with a black top. The ships of the Guion Line had black funnels with a red band near the top (though not at the very top). Inman Line ships also had black funnels, with a wide white band around them.

The funnels themselves also changed in design. As ships grew larger and faster, they required larger powerplants to operate them. This necessitated the addition of more boilers, which in turn required a second (and later third and fourth) funnel to ventilate. Shipping lines also frequently made these funnels larger than what was required, to make their vessel look more impressive.

Cunard's *Campania* and *Lucania* were said to have the largest funnels in the world when they were put into service in 1893. Though large funnels had the benefit of helping to keep smoke and soot off the open deck spaces, the scale of these ships' funnels was exaggerated in comparison to the size of the ship.

The size of the vessel was largely dependent on where it was expected to be sailing. The economics of the Atlantic passage allowed for the growth of passenger ships to huge sizes. The proliferation of commercial ventures between Europe and the USA, as well as the relatively short distances involved, led to the building of large express liners.

Ships built to service smaller and less-developed ports, and those built to transit enclosed waterways, such as the Suez Canal, had to be built to fit those waterways. This limited their size. The early Holland America (NASM) liners, *Rotterdam* and *Maas*, were built to fit the Voorne Canal. Once the Nieuwe Waterweg was completed, Holland America was able to build bigger ships.

It was the express liners that often received the vast majority of the media attention as the various shipping lines sought to outdo each other in terms of size and speed. But there were large numbers of intermediate ships plying these routes as well. These intermediate liners were built for economy over speed. Sometimes they were purpose-built for the intermediate route, and sometimes they were simply services run by superseded express liners, making them slower than the premium service.

Great Britain (1845–86). Anti-fouling paint is used on parts of the hull that would most often make contact with the water. This helps to reduce the build-up of marine life on the hull, which impacts the efficiency of a ship. (Frame & Cross)

Opposite: *Oceanic* (1899–1914). *Oceanic* was a significant ship for White Star Line as it helped the company cement their position as a leading transatlantic line. Designed to offer greater passenger comforts at the expense of speed, the vessel was longer than Brunel's *Great Eastern*. (Henderson & Cremer Collection)

Clockwise from top left: *Austral* (1882–1903). Fancy dress days were a common activity aboard ocean liners in an age before organised cruise activities. This scene from aboard *Austral* shows the benefits of the covered awnings, which helped shade passengers from the sun. (Henderson & Cremer Collection); *Austral* (1882–1903). The radial davits of *Austral*'s lifeboats can be seen in this view looking forward along her top deck. The ship's engines were supplemented by sails, which were hoisted when the winds were favourable. (Henderson & Cremer Collection); *Orizaba* (1886–1905). Passing the time during long line voyages often led to long days spent on deck. Aboard *Orizaba*, canvas awnings were erected to offer shelter from the sun. Despite travelling in hot, tropical weather, passengers still dressed in traditional northern hemisphere attire. (Henderson & Cremer Collection)

Etruria (1884–1908). *Etruria* and her sister *Umbria* were single-screw liners, with twin stacks. The ships were coal powered and utilised reciprocating engines to drive their screw. (Henderson & Cremer Collection)

Umbria (1884–1908). *Umbria* and her sister *Etruria* were the largest and fastest liners of their day. Despite capturing the speed record numerous times for the fastest transatlantic crossing, the ships could also both make way under sail power. (Henderson & Cremer Collection)

Boat trains in Napoli. Railway services were an integral part of the passenger ship experience, being employed to carry passengers and the mails to and from coastal ports. In this image, Orient Line's special Napoli Boulogne service is pulling into the station. (Henderson & Cremer Collection)

Intermediate liners would often stop in multiple ports, or run to alternative ports, such as Boston or Halifax over New York. As time went on, some of these superseded ships were also sent cruising.

A cruise ship, or one undertaking coastal voyages, was not expected to run into the worst waves or weather. Though they could and did get pummelled by storms, they weren't out in the open ocean, facing these dangers a long way from aid.

Transocean ships, and especially transatlantic liners, needed to be built to cope regularly with these conditions. To that end they were built with very strong bows and tanked-in forward superstructures that helped protect them from the large waves and rough weather frequently experienced on the Northern Atlantic route. These necessary safety features gave them a look that was very distinctive.

Equally distinctive were the features built into ships that transited multiple ports during their journeys, such as the ships of the Messageries Maritimes.

Though speed was important for these ships, they had more port stops than the Atlantic liners. This allowed them to trade with a greater number of places, meaning that they often loaded and offloaded cargo at the various ports they visited. They also took much longer to complete a single voyage.

The Messageries Maritimes steamship *Natal*, for example, took forty days in 1883 to get from Marseilles to Adelaide, compared with the White Star Line's *Germanic*, which undertook the summer transatlantic crossing from Liverpool to New York in eight and a half days. The distances involved were very different, and the number of stops was also widely disparate.

Germanic's crossing had a single call at Queenstown, now Cobh, in Ireland on her way to New York. *Natal* sailed via Port Said, Suez, Aden, Mahé, Mauritius and Réunion before reaching Adelaide. She then went on to Melbourne, Sydney and Noumea. The many ports of call allowed ships such as *Natal* to trade along the way, rather than just at either end of the voyage.

To allow for easy cargo stowage and removal, ships were fitted with derricks near their cargo areas. These were more obvious on some ships, and less obvious on others, often depending on how frequently they were used during a journey.

Even with the potential for cargo and passenger trade, as well as the mail contracts, shipbuilding was still an expensive business. With the increase in competition on all routes, shipping lines needed to continue to build new tonnage in order to remain competitive.

To finance their new builds, shipping lines could attempt capital-raising endeavours from their shareholders, and often sought loans from either banks, other businesses or their government.

The British Empire had long held a dominance on many of the established shipping routes. Numerous early transatlantic shipping lines had been based in Britain, including Great Western Steamship Company, Cunard, Guion Line and White Star Line. The largest shipping company in the world in 1890 was P&O, also a British company. But lines from other countries were beginning to catch up.

In 1890 the second-largest shipping company was Norddeutscher Lloyd, with the International Navigation Company, based in America, beginning to consolidate shipping lines under their ownership, including the Inman Line.

The military potential of the merchant shipping fleet was obvious to the governments of many European nations, including the British Admiralty. In sheer numbers alone, British merchant shipping had the potential to bolster the Navy significantly in a wartime scenario.

During the Crimean War a number of British-flagged ships, including those of the Cunard Line and P&O, were requisitioned for service by the British Admiralty. The German Empire had also seen the potential for using merchant ships as military transports, with fourteen Norddeutscher Lloyd liners requisitioned as troop transports during the Boxer Rebellion in China in 1900.

With increasing tensions in Europe throughout the end of the nineteenth century and into the beginning of the twentieth century, the various governments began to take a serious interest in the expansion of the shipping lines based in their country. This resulted in a period of rapid growth for many of the European-based shipping companies.

The government involvement in merchant shipbuilding led to new design requirements in the new builds. As one of the terms of providing a loan for the building of new ships, the British government, for example, required that new ships be built to military specifications. This was known as the British Auxiliary Armed Merchant Cruiser Agreement.

This didn't necessarily mean that the ships were built as military vessels, fitted with guns and armour plating. Rather the ships needed to meet certain requirements when it came to size and dimensions, as well as having the capacity to be fitted with armaments should the need arise.

Opposite page: Clockwise from top left:
Kaiser Wilhelm der Grosse (1897–1914). The first of the four-stackers, *Kaiser Wilhelm der Grosse* captured the transatlantic speed record and inaugurated a European trend of building large, four-funnelled express liners. (Bill Miller Collection); *Kaiser Wilhelm der Grosse* (1897–1914). The first-class smoking room aboard *Kaiser Wilhelm der Grosse* illustrates how far shipboard luxuries had come by 1897. Sheltered from the elements, the room was richly decorated and even offered natural light thanks to a built-in skylight. (Michael W. Pocock/www.maritimequest. com); *Deutschland* (1900–25). *Deutschland* was Hamburg-Amerika's first four-funnelled liner. The ship featured an ornate first-class interior, with a dining room that spanned three decks and included a viewing area. (Michael W. Pocock/www.maritimequest.com)

Teutonic (1889–1921). The White Star Line's *Teutonic* shows off improvements in design, with a large, centralised superstructure and two well-balanced funnels. The ship was built to armed merchant cruiser specifications and was toured by Kaiser Wilhelm II in 1899. (Henderson & Cremer Collection)

In 1891 Cunard took advantage of government loans to commission two new express liners, *Campania* and *Lucania*. The ships entered service in 1893 at 12,950 grt each. They were the largest ships then afloat, and the fastest, with *Campania* and then *Lucania* successively capturing the transatlantic speed records. They were twin-screw ships, powered by enormous triple-expansion engines, and had a service speed of 22 knots.

In the German Empire, Kaiser Wilhelm II had convinced the two largest German shipping lines to build bigger ships for the Atlantic passage under a similar agreement to that in Britain. In response, Norddeutscher Lloyd built the first of the 'four stackers', *Kaiser Wilhem der Grosse*.

In addition to having four funnels, *Kaiser Wilhelm der Grosse* was 191.2m (627.29ft) long, eclipsing the length of Cunard's *Lucania* by more than a metre, and making it the largest ship in service. She was also a very fast ship, taking the speed records from the Cunard ships.

She would not hold the records for long, with the larger White Star Liner *Oceanic* entering service in 1899 and the faster Hamburg-Amerika liner *Deutschland* arriving in 1900.

6

BIGGER, BETTER, STRONGER

In 1897 the Spithead Naval Review, for Queen Victoria's Diamond Jubilee, was interrupted when a small vessel zipped through the lines of assembled ships, outrunning the naval vessels attempting to stop it. That vessel was the *Turbinia* and it ushered in a new development for steamships.

Charles Parsons had spent years developing the steam turbine as a new and improved way to generate motive power. The Parsons turbine was invented in 1884 and, after refining the technology, Parsons attempted to sell his invention to the British Navy, but they paid little attention. His stunt with the turbine-powered *Turbinia* at the Naval Review forced them to take notice.

While the Navy was the first to adopt the turbine to power their ships, it wasn't long before passenger shipping started to follow suit. *Victorian* was launched in 1904 for the Montreal Ocean Steamship Company, better known as the Allan Line, and was the first turbine-powered ocean liner. She was fitted with three-screw propellers, which were driven directly by three Parsons turbines, one high pressure on the centre shaft, and two low pressure on the wing shafts. It was reported that *Victorian* reached 19.5 knots during her sea trials. *Victorian* was joined by a sister ship, *Virginian*, and the two were employed between the United Kingdom and Canada as mail ships.

Other recent innovations were also coming of age in a maritime setting. The Marconi wireless had been invented in 1895 and in 1900 *Kaiser Wilhelm der Grosse* was fitted with the technology during a refit. *Lucania* and *Campania* were both fitted with wireless rooms during 1901 and made history when they transmitted the first ice bulletin by wireless.

Lucania was also used by Guglielmo Marconi in 1903 to conduct some of his experiments in wireless technology, staying in contact with radio stations throughout the Atlantic crossing. From 10 October that year *Lucania* published an on-board news sheet, the *Cunard Daily Bulletin*, based on radio communications the ship had been undertaking during the day.

Lucania was also one of the first ships fitted with submarine signalling in 1905. Submarine signalling used underwater acoustic signals for communications. Designed by the Submarine Signal Company and licensed by Norddeutsche Maschinenund Armaturenfabrik for use in Europe, submarine signalling ushered in a new level of marine safety.

Fixed points, such as underwater hazards, could be fitted with the signals, to warn ships that they were there. The signals were also employed on lightships, and within ports. Ship-to-ship signalling, such as the technology installed aboard *Lucania*, also allowed for vessels to communicate their location with each other. This allowed them to operate with greater safety and efficiency even when visibility was low, for example when they were transiting fogbanks, but this was only useful if both ships were fitted with the technology.

Meanwhile, new lines were entering the cruising market. In 1904 P&O converted their ship *Rome* for full-time cruising. *Rome* had been used on their Australian mail service from 1881, and was an iron-hulled, single-screw steamer. Following her cruise conversion in 1904 she was renamed *Vectis* and sailed from London to destinations including Norway, the Baltic, the Canary Islands and the Adriatic Sea. P&O partnered with Thomas Cook to organise shore excursions in *Vectis*'s ports of call.

In 1905 Cunard brought their first turbine-powered ship into service, *Carmania*. *Carmania* was 198.2m (650.4ft) long and 19,566 grt with three propellers. Cunard also built a sister ship, *Caronia*, which shared a very similar design, though only had two propellers and was powered using reciprocating engines.

The *Carmania* and *Caronia* were a test of sorts, allowing Cunard to prove for themselves that the benefits offered by the turbine were worth the investment in retraining their engineers to service the new technology. *Carmania* proved the turbine's superiority, being able to achieve higher speeds more economically. Cunard was already building their next generation of express liners, designed with turbines, and the success of *Carmania* helped confirm their decision.

Lusitania and *Mauretania* were to be the biggest ships in the world when launched. They were the first turbine-powered ships to capture the transatlantic speed record and were able to achieve speeds of 24 knots. Built with the aid of a £2.6 million loan, the ships were built at two separate yards. *Lusitania* was built at John Brown Shipyard in Clydebank and *Mauretania* was built by Swan Hunter & Wigham Richardson in Newcastle, with both entering service in 1907.

The new turbine technology was not without its teething problems. *Lusitania*, which entered service first, had to be sent back to her builder to have strengthening beams added. This was a result of significant vibrations, caused by the operation of her turbines and propellers when run at high speeds. *Mauretania*, which was still being completed, was also given strengthening beams by her shipyard.

Lusitania captured the westbound and eastbound speed records in October of 1907, before being eclipsed by *Mauretania*, which took the eastbound record in 1907 and the westbound record in 1909.

The year 1909 would prove an important one for the Marconi wireless, with the White Star liner *Republic* using it to make a CQD call (all stations – distress) on 23 January. The Lloyd Italiano liner *Florida* had collided with *Republic* in the early hours of the morning, causing significant damage to *Republic*. The signal was received by the Siasconset land station, on Nantucket, Massachusetts, and relayed to the White Star liner *Baltic*, along with a number of other liners. *Florida* managed to return to the *Republic* and took aboard those passengers and crew who had been evacuated, despite their ship also being damaged in the collision.

Lucania (1893–1909). *Lucania* was a twin-screw liner powered by giant reciprocating engines. Her external appearance included two oversized funnels and twin masts that could not be rigged for sails. (Henderson & Cremer Collection)

Celtic (1901–28). *Celtic* was one of White Star Line's 'Big Four'. At over 20,900 grt, she was the first ship to exceed *Great Eastern*'s tonnage. Each subsequent liner of the class, *Cedric*, *Baltic* and *Adriatic*, improved on the design of *Celtic*. (Henderson & Cremer Collection)

Baltic (1904–33). *Baltic* was the third ship in White Star Line's 'Big Four'. In 1909 she was involved in rescuing passengers and crew of the stricken liner *Republic*. (Henderson & Cremer Collection)

Opposite page: Clockwise from left:
Vectis (1881–1912). Originally put into service as the *Rome*, this ship was built for line voyages and carried Winston Churchill in 1897. (Henderson & Cremer Collection); *Vectis* (1881–1912). Following a refit in 1904, the former *Rome* was renamed *Vectis* and sent cruising. P&O engaged Thomas Cook to manage the shore excursions during the ship's cruising years. (Henderson & Cremer Collection); *Carmania* (1905–32). Cunard's *Carmania* was not designed to capture the records for size or speed. Fitted with steam turbines, she established a Cunard trend of using turbines that would endure until *QE2* in 1967. (Henderson & Cremer Collection)

Adriatic (1907–35). The last of the 'Big Four', *Adriatic* introduced unique amenities including a Turkish bath. She was slightly smaller than the *Kaiserin Auguste Victoria* and was superseded by *Lusitania* and *Mauretania* in both size and luxury in the year she entered service. (Henderson & Cremer Collection)

When *Baltic* arrived on the scene the passengers from both *Republic* and *Florida* were transferred. *Florida* and *Baltic* were able to make way to New York, and attempts were made to save *Republic*, but she foundered and sank later that evening.

Later that year another ship, *Arapahoe*, used wireless to make the distress signal SOS after her propeller shaft snapped, leaving her helpless. The signal was received by the Cape Hatteras Marconi station in North Carolina and assistance was sent.

In 1910 the Orient liner *Otranto* made history when she sent a wireless message to HMS *Powerful*. The message travelled an incredible 3,218km from *Otranto*, off the coast of Fremantle in Western Australia, to *Powerful*, in Sydney.

But a ship was already under construction that would change the face of shipping forever, in a way that its owners did not foresee.

In 1910 White Star Line launched their biggest ship yet, the *Olympic*. *Olympic* was 269.1m (882ft) long and 45,324 grt. Built at Harland & Wolff in Belfast, this ship was to be the first in a trio of ships all named after ancient Greek mythology. The second ship in the class, *Titanic*, had been laid down in 1909 at the same shipyard and it was this ship that would go down in maritime history, though not for good reasons.

Like her sister ship, *Olympic*, *Titanic* was fitted with a combination of triple-expansion engines and a low-pressure turbine, which solved the issues the Cunarders had faced with excessive vibrations. She was luxuriously appointed, with first-class spaces being some of the finest of the day. She was also a very large ship, the same length as *Olympic*, though with a slightly larger tonnage, owing to the enclosing of part of the B deck promenade to build the Café Parisien as well as enclosing the forward half of the A deck promenade.

DID YOU KNOW?

Aquitania carried 100,000 pieces of china and earthenware, 26,000 pieces of silver and 100,000 pieces of linen.

First-class passengers on *Titanic* had access to a Turkish bath and a gym as well as the specialty extra-tariff restaurant, Café Parisien. Select first-class cabins had their own en suite and the two parlour suites had their own private promenade spaces.

The ill-fated maiden voyage of *Titanic* departed on 10 April 1912. The ship left from Southampton and made calls at Cherbourg and Queenstown, before heading across the Atlantic. On 14 April 1912, at 11:40 p.m., the ship struck an iceberg, sustaining damage to six of her watertight compartments. The ship sank at 2:20 a.m. on 15 April 1912, with significant loss of life. The loss of *Titanic* had a profound impact on both sides of the Atlantic.

Following the sinking, inquiries were held in both Britain and America. Through these hearings many inadequacies in the regulations surrounding shipboard safety were identified.

One of the most well-known issues brought to light by the *Titanic* disaster was the lack of life-preservation equipment aboard, and the lack of training in how to use it. *Titanic* did not carry enough lifeboats for all aboard. Furthermore, there had been no lifeboat drill carried out on the ship, with some surviving crew members reporting that they didn't know how many passengers could be safely carried in the lifeboats.

The number of lifeboats required to be carried by a ship at that time had been determined by the tonnage of the ship, rather than by the number of persons the ship was able to carry. *Titanic* fell under the regulations set by the British Board of Trade. The regulations had a top bracket for vessels of more than 10,000 grt. *Titanic* was 46,329 grt, more than four and a half times that size. She actually carried more lifeboats than was required for a vessel of her size, but with a capacity of only 1,178, this number still fell well short of being able to accommodate all on board.

In addition to recommendations to update the lifeboat requirements, the inquiries also made strong suggestions for other safety updates. The Atlantic ice fields began to be monitored and patrolled, with a view to informing shipping of dangerous icebergs. The International Ice Patrol was officially established in 1914, operated by the United States government, but funded by thirteen nations.

Mauretania (1907–35). *Mauretania* was the pride of England, having been built at the Swan Hunter & Wigham Richardson yard in Newcastle. She was also renowned as the world's fastest liner throughout the 1910s and '20s. (Henderson & Cremer Collection)

Otranto (1909–18). The ornate finishings of *Otranto*'s first-class lounge were designed to echo land-based luxury. (Henderson & Cremer Collection)

Otranto (1909–18). Built for the Australian run, *Otranto* undertook this service until the outbreak of the First World War. She was lost in 1918 after colliding with P&O's *Kashmir*. (Henderson & Cremer Collection)

Olympic (1911–35). The first in the Olympic-class liners, *Olympic* was the only ship of the trio to enjoy a long service career. After the *Titanic* disaster, *Olympic* was retrofitted to carry additional lifeboats, which are seen here along her entire boat deck length. (Henderson & Cremer Collection)

Boat drill aboard P&O Liner. This is an important part of safety of life at sea. For over a century now, this has involved donning of lifejackets and mustering to lifeboat stations or muster stations. (Henderson & Cremer Collection)

Aquitania (1914–50). Seen here in her original configuration, the *Aquitania* was the largest four-funnelled liner ever built. Her design features a clean bow, devoid of a well deck, with a superstructure that is bulkier than that aboard *Lusitania* and *Mauretania*. (Henderson & Cremer Collection)

Vaterland (1914–38). One of the Ballin trio of liners, Hamburg-Amerika's *Vaterland* was the world's largest liner when she entered service. Her German operations were short-lived, with the ship running trooping services for America during the First World War. (Michael W. Pocock/www.maritimequest.com)

Vaterland (1914–38). *Vaterland*'s design included an inboard lifeboat deck from her midships aft. (Michael W. Pocock/ www.maritimequest.com)

DID YOU KNOW?

The day before *Aquitania*'s maiden voyage departed, the Canadian Pacific liner, *Empress of Ireland*, was involved in a collision with the *Storstad*. *Empress of Ireland* sank in fourteen minutes, with a loss of 1,012 lives.

The Marconi Wireless, for years used primarily to send messages and for commercial gain, also became an integral part of safety operations. *Titanic*'s wireless operators had managed to contact *Carpathia* largely by luck. *Carpathia*'s wireless operator had actually finished work for the day when he decided to check the communications one final time before bed. On the night of the sinking there were several ships closer to *Titanic* than *Carpathia*, but their wireless rooms were unattended at the time, and they did not receive notifications of the ship's fate until morning.

The inquiries recommended that radio rooms on ships be sufficiently staffed to allow them to be operated twenty-four hours a day. They were also required to be fitted with a secondary power supply, not dependent on the vessel's main power supplies. In the United States the 1912 amendment to the Wireless Ship Act of 1910 and the Radio Act of 1912 brought these two recommendations into law.

Titanic's sister ship *Olympic* was returned to her builders in October 1912 to be retrofitted with significant safety improvements. This included adding forty-eight additional lifeboats as well as creating a double hull inside the boiler and engine rooms. Five of her watertight bulkheads were extended higher in the ship, providing better protection in case of a hull breach, and an additional bulkhead was added to protect the electrical dynamo room.

Olympic was also given some other upgrades, including adding a Café Parisien and additional first-class accommodation. With her new configuration, *Olympic* had grown in tonnage and was now larger than her ill-fated sister.

In Germany, Hamburg-Amerika was building a ship to challenge the size and speed of the British liners. *Imperator* entered service in 1913. The ship had been altered somewhat during construction to increase the safety features aboard. She was given a double hull and twelve watertight bulkheads, and the lifeboat capacity was increased to 5,500, enough for more people than the ship would travel with.

The ship was fitted with Yarrow water tube boilers. Water tube boilers had been in use on locomotives and also on naval vessels since the early 1900s, but they hadn't been widely adopted in passenger shipping. The older fire tube boiler design of the Scotch marine boilers was well trusted, but the water tube design was shown to be more efficient.

Imperator was given a very opulent fit out, with numerous public spaces available for her first-, second- and even third-class passengers. A total of 1,700 of her total passenger capacity of 4,200 were able to be housed in the less-desirable steerage-class locations aboard the ship.

Though *Imperator* impressed with her size and opulence, she suffered a significant listing problem when manoeuvring and was not considered a very stable ship in open ocean. In 1913 the ship was returned to its builders for remedial works, which determined that the centre of gravity was too high. To remedy this problem the ship's three funnels were shortened by 3m (9ft 10in), heavy furniture was removed and replaced with wicker, while marble, which had been used extensively throughout the first-class areas, was likewise removed. Some 2,000 tons of cement was also poured into the ship's double bottom, to further lower the centre of gravity. During these works a fire sprinkler system was also added to the ship.

Cunard introduced their newest express liner, *Aquitania*, in May 1914. Slightly shorter than *Imperator*, *Aquitania* became known for her interior design, which was considered both grand and elegant, comfortable and welcoming.

Like *Imperator*, *Aquitania* had been given a double hull and watertight bulkheads. She had enough lifeboats for all persons on board, two of which were motorised and fitted with Marconi wireless.

In Germany, Hamburg-Amerika was working on their newest ship, *Vaterland*. Though not yet completed, this was to be the largest ship in the world, bigger than both *Imperator* and *Aquitania*, at 54,282 grt.

In 1914 the first International Convention for the Safety of Life at Sea (SOLAS) was agreed. This set the minimum standards for construction, safety equipment and operations of merchant vessels. The introduction of SOLAS was a direct outcome of the *Titanic* disaster. But the enactment of this agreement was interrupted by the outbreak of the First World War in July 1914.

THE SHIP AS THE LIFEBOAT

When *Titanic* foundered on 15 April 1912, over 1,500 people died. This horrendous death toll was largely attributed to the ship having insufficient lifeboat capacity for all those aboard, and rescue ships being too far away to render aid before *Titanic* sank.

However, the purpose of a lifeboat was fundamentally different in 1912 to what it is today, and practical experience at the time supported allowing ships to sail without enough boats for all.

The early twentieth century saw huge leaps in the size of passenger ships. As ships grew, naval architects worked hard to ensure that each successive generation was safer than the designs that came before. With the widespread use of watertight bulkheads, passenger ships were deemed capable of remaining afloat for longer durations, even when they had sustained unrecoverable damage.

Wireless radio, Morse lamps and distress rockets meant that if a ship was in distress, it had a way to contact those around it. The busy shipping lanes established across the world's oceans led authorities to believe that any large ship in distress would quickly be able to establish contact with nearby vessels, who would then render aid.

In essence, the ship had become its own lifeboat. If damaged, the watertight compartments would keep the ship afloat. If severely damaged, the compartments would slow the sinking to such a pace that assistance would surely arrive in time.

In this scenario, the ship's lifeboat was never intended to be filled to capacity, lowered and left in the ocean as a primary means to escape a sinking ship. Rather, the lifeboat was a method of transporting passengers and crew from the stricken yet still afloat liner to nearby ships that had come to help. The lifeboats would ferry back and forth to transport all passengers and crew during an evacuation.

Interestingly, this theory was deemed to be a safety improvement in the Edwardian era. There had been many instances of lifeboats being lowered from a sinking ship, only to be lost to storms, rough waves, or fogbanks. Most shipwrecks do not happen on clear, still nights as witnessed on the night *Titanic* sank. They usually occur in bad weather, with heavy rain, high winds, rough seas, and poor visibility.

Open-topped, wooden, unmotorised lifeboats would not last long in such conditions. It was considered safer to ensure the ship remained seaworthy for as long as possible, than to risk lowering boats without the certainty of nearby aid.

The theory of using a ship as its own lifeboat was 'proven' sound in 1909 when *Republic* collided with *Florida*. While *Florida* remained afloat, *Republic* was severely damaged. *Republic*'s watertight compartments held up long enough to allow an orderly evacuation to nearby vessels. The six people that did perish died in the collision rather than the sinking.

It is this practical example that gave designers and shipping lines the confidence to continue to pursue this philosophy up until 15 April 1912, when it was tragically proven to be flawed. *Titanic* is famously remembered as the ship without enough lifeboats, but it's important to remember that nearly all her contemporaries followed the same safety principles, and the flaws in this logic weren't clear to designers, ship owners or their crews until the unthinkable happened.

7

BAD TIMES AND GOOD TIMES

The outbreak of war had a profound impact on passenger shipping. While passenger and cargo ships continued to operate relatively normally during the early days of the war, as the conflict escalated, this became increasingly difficult.

There was an immediate decrease in the civilian freight market, which persisted throughout the war. At the same time, costs skyrocketed, and ships began to be taken up from service by their governments. The lack of tonnage further exacerbated the freight difficulties and also put strain on the ability of shipping companies to service their mail contracts.

Work on passenger ships that were under construction at the time, such as White Star's *Britannic* and P&O's *Naldera* and *Narkunda*, was impacted, as resources were diverted to military contracts. Coal became scarce and the docks were understaffed, leading to further issues with income.

Ships requisitioned by their governments could be required for several different uses, some of them coming with much higher likelihood of loss.

The German liner *Kaiser Wilhelm der Grosse* was put into service as an auxiliary cruiser very early in the war. Painted in grey and black and fitted with weapons, it was sent into battle. After sinking three enemy vessels, the ship was scuttled in August 1914 by her crew when she ran out of ammunition while engaging with the British cruiser HMS *Highflyer*.

A number of British steamers were also lost to enemy action while under requisition as armed merchant cruisers, including P&O's *India*.

Though many British-flagged passenger ships were initially placed on the armed merchant cruiser list, and some even converted to armed merchant cruisers, most of the passenger ships fairly quickly proved unsuitable for this use. They had high fuel consumption and were too large to be able to manoeuvre easily.

Instead, these requisitioned passenger ships often found use as troop carriers and hospital ships, for which they were much better suited. The conversions these ships underwent removed most of the luxuries for which the ship was known and replaced them with fittings better suited for their new roles.

Ships converted for trooping duties, such as Cunard's *Mauretania*, had additional berths added, to allow the ship to carry more troops at one time. The faster and more modern passenger liners were often considered good ships to be assigned to by the troops, as they were believed to be both safer and ofttimes more comfortable to travel aboard.

Britannic, the third ship in White Star's Olympic class, had not even entered passenger service when she was requisitioned as a hospital ship. Her original layout would have been similar to *Olympic*'s peacetime design, but the changes that were made to operate her as a hospital ship were great. These included converting her first-class dining room and reception room into operating theatres, while her hull was painted white with a horizontal green stripe and large red cross on the side. *Britannic* would not survive the war, hitting an underwater mine off the coast of Kea, Greece, in November 1916.

But it was not just the ships actively involved in the war effort that were in danger. With no alternative mode of transport, passenger and mail ships were still required to operate their usual routes, sometimes under government mandate.

Cunard's *Lusitania* was one such ship to continue operating a passenger service across the Atlantic during the war. Though the liner had been placed on the armed merchant cruiser list, she had never been called into service. The British government placed considerable pressure on Cunard to maintain their passenger service, though it was considerably scaled back from the line's usual operations.

Lusitania operated with a different look to what she had sported prior to the war. The ship's funnels were painted black, and she flew no flag while in the war zone. Despite a printed threat from the Imperial German Embassy in many American newspapers, the ship was still sailing with a large complement of passengers when it was struck off Ireland by a torpedo fired by *U-20* on 7 May 1915. The ship sank in eighteen minutes, with the loss of 1,198 lives. The disaster served to reinforce the message of how dangerous the waters, particularly around Europe, had become.

Throughout the war, there were huge losses, both in people and in shipping tonnage. P&O, for example, lost twenty-five ships, with a combined tonnage of 186,703, during the war, which also claimed the lives of 258 staff. And they were not alone in their losses. No shipping company was untouched by the war.

While the armistice was declared on 11 November 1918, it would take years for passenger shipping to recover. Many merchant ships remained in military service for months after the war ended, used to repatriate troops. The German shipping lines had been decimated, with their largest ships being transferred to their British and American competitors as war reparations.

But these ships were not in the same condition they had been in prior to the war. They still required refurbishment to bring them back to a standard fit for paying passengers. This process took time, as resources remained scarce and there were not enough dockyards or workers to complete all the works at one time.

Not all of the shipping lines survived the war years. Some of the smaller lines were snapped up by bigger concerns, with P&O in particular purchasing an interest in a number of other companies. In addition to purchasing much of the shares of the New Zealand Shipping Company and the Union Steamship Company of New Zealand, they also acquired a controlling interest in the Orient Line, Khedivial Mail Company and the General Steam Navigation Company during the war years. Additionally, they entered into a joint venture with the British India Steamship Company to purchase the Hain Steamship Company.

But as things around the world began to return to a new state of normal, the major shipping lines slowly began to recover. On the North Atlantic, Cunard were able to quickly re-establish themselves as the pre-eminent line, returning *Mauretania* and *Aquitania* to their express service along with the ex-Hamburg-Amerika liner *Imperator*. After a year in service under her German name, *Imperator* was given a full refit and converted from coal to oil burning. She was also given the name *Berengaria*.

Their major competitors, White Star Line, were not so lucky. White Star Line's three-ship service was in tatters. *Titanic* had been lost prior to the war, and *Britannic* lost during the war, leaving only *Olympic* to re-enter service. White Star Line had purchased the as yet incomplete Hamburg-Amerika liner *Bismarck* to replace *Britannic*.

The ship was renamed *Majestic*, and work was recommenced on the liner to get her ready for service. She was converted to run on oil rather than coal, but the fitting out of the ship did not go smoothly. The ship was damaged by fire on 5 October 1920, delaying her entry into service. She eventually became operational for White Star in 1922, joining *Olympic* and *Homeric* (the former Norddeutscher Lloyd liner *Columbus*).

Compagnie Générale Transatlantique (also known as CGT and the French Line) were able to complete their ship *Paris*, which had been laid down in 1913, but did not enter service until 1921. *Paris* contained many luxuries, which until this point had been rare on transatlantic liners. This included private telephones in first-class staterooms, and square windows, rather than the traditional portholes. Her interiors were also a blend of styles, from the more traditional to the modern.

Paris was a success, and the French Line began building the next in the fleet, *Île de France*, in 1925. She was decorated almost entirely in art deco style, setting her apart from her contemporaries. The ship had many passenger amenities, including a shooting gallery, and a carousel for children. The décor aboard *Île de France* would inspire passenger ships for the next two decades, as well as helping to influence the design of many buildings.

Though built to service the same mail contract as the earlier *Paris*, *Île de France* was designed to carry far fewer passengers. This was due to the significant decrease in steerage passengers over the years since *Paris* had entered service.

In 1921 the United States implemented the Emergency Quota Act, which introduced immigration quotas, thus restricting the number of people able to emigrate to the United States based on country of origin. This act was introduced due to the high rates of unemployment in America following the First World War.

The Immigration Act of 1924 further restricted the numbers of people allowed to immigrate and made a big impact on the numbers of passengers being carried by the ocean liners. Steerage and third class were far less populated than they had been in the previous decades, since there was no longer a reason for many of the people that would have travelled in this class previously to travel at all.

As steerage passengers had long been the financial backbone of the transatlantic shipping companies, this left them in a quandary. With a significant decrease in the numbers of passengers heading westbound, ship owners had to find new markets to make up the shortfall or risk financial ruin. This was especially necessary during the quieter seasons.

But it wasn't all bad news. The 1920s also brought with it prosperity in the western world, leading to an increase in affluence and thus growth in the appeal of cruise holidays. The decade also brought Prohibition in the United States, leading to the emergence of 'booze cruises to nowhere'. These voyages were undertaken by foreign-flagged vessels from American ports. The ships would sail into international waters where American travellers could legally enjoy access to alcohol – something they were unable to do at home.

Lusitania (1907–15). *Lusitania* was one of Cunard's fast express liners, bested only by *Mauretania* in terms of speed. During the First World War she ran a reduced passenger service on the Atlantic and was lost in May 1915 when torpedoed by a German U-boat. (Henderson & Cremer Collection)

Empress of Britain (1906–30). *Empress of Britain* was one of many ships requisitioned for wartime service. Like many others in the First World War, she wore dazzle in an attempt to confuse enemy shipping. (Michael W. Pocock/www.maritimequest.com)

Opposite page:
Top: *New York* (1888–1923). The *New York* was used as a troop transport from 1918. This ship was involved in an incident during *Titanic*'s maiden voyage that almost resulted in a collision between the two ships. (Michael W. Pocock/www.maritimequest.com)
Bottom: *Leviathan* (1914–38). *Vaterland* was seized by the Americans when they entered the war. Renamed *Leviathan*, the ship sailed on trooping duties and later sailed for United States Lines. (Michael W. Pocock/www.maritimequest.com)

Berengaria (1912–39). Originally entering service as Hamburg-Amerika's *Imperator*, *Berengaria* was acquired by Cunard as war reparations for the loss of *Lusitania*. She differed from the Cunard express liners in that she only had three funnels. (Henderson & Cremer Collection)

Majestic (1922–39). Designed as the world's largest liner, and intended to be named *Bismark*, *Majestic* was the flagship of the White Star Line. The incomplete ship was acquired by White Star as war reparations for the loss of *Britannic*. (Henderson & Cremer Collection)

Homeric (1913–36). Originally built as the Norddeutscher Lloyd liner *Columbus*, *Homeric* was acquired by White Star Line after the First World War. The ship was paired with *Olympic* and *Majestic* on the transatlantic express service. (Henderson & Cremer Collection)

Île de France (1926–59). The three-funnelled *Île de France* is trailed by the four-funnelled *Aquitania* during their Second World War trooping service. (Henderson & Cremer Collection)

Carinthia (1925–40). *Carinthia* inaugurated the first Cunard cruise in Australia, which occurred during her 1925 world cruise. A single-funnelled intermediate liner, the ship was lost during the Second World War. (Henderson & Cremer Collection)

Ranchi (1925–53). As cruising grew in popularity, shipping lines sent more ships on pleasure voyages. *Ranchi* was one such example, cruising between 1926 and 1929. (Henderson & Cremer Collection)

Mauretania (1907–35). *Mauretania* went cruising towards the end of her career and was painted white to reduce the heat that was absorbed by her traditionally painted black hull. (Henderson & Cremer Collection)

Pleasure cruising also helped improve profitability. Royal Mail Line's newly acquired 16,063-grt *Orca* undertook a series of cruises from 1923. These voyages took place in the winter season and travelled to the warmer climates of the tropical Caribbean.

World cruising, of a style modern cruise passengers would recognise, saw its first widespread success in 1922 when the Cunard Line's *Laconia* set sail on her inaugural circumnavigation.

The voyage was undertaken in partnership with American Express, who oversaw the ticket sales and worked with Cunard to develop an itinerary that retraced many historic locations visited by the Magellan expedition.

Third-class berths wouldn't sell well for a pleasure voyage, so *Laconia*'s third class, which could accommodate 1,500 passengers, was decommissioned for the journey. American Express sold the cruise in both first and second class, limiting the total carriage aboard the ship to several hundred passengers.

Laconia's world cruise was exclusively a northern hemisphere affair, sailing only as far south as Singapore and Panama. The voyage utilised the Panama Canal, which had only been operational for eight years, as well as transiting the Suez Canal.

In 1923 several other ships set sail on world cruises, including Cunard's *Samaria* and Canadian Pacific's *Empress of France*, as well as the United American Lines' *Resolute*. Their voyages paved the way for future world cruises throughout the 1920s.

Royal Mail Line's *Orca* made headlines when it called at South African ports in 1926, offering the first cruise holidays for that region.

Also in 1926, P&O's 16,651-grt liner *Ranchi* was transformed for cruising. Buoyed by the success of earlier cruise voyages, P&O sent *Ranchi* on a series of Mediterranean and North Sea cruises in the summer of 1926, returning good income. This pleased the P&O board of directors and management, leading to the ship undertaking numerous summer cruises until 1929.

Holland America Line entered the cruise business in 1926, with their first cruise taking place aboard the 1922-built 15,450-grt *Veendam*. This pioneering voyage departed New York and sailed to the Caribbean.

While there had been few new builds completed for passenger service during the war years, there had been learnings taken from the way the many different ships being operated had performed.

New passenger ships being designed were to be given new features. In November 1927 the *Augustus*, which had been built for Navigazione Generale Italiana, departed on her maiden voyage. She was the largest diesel ship of her day.

Even before *Augustus* entered into service, White Star Line had ordered a diesel ship of their own. A new *Britannic* was laid down in April of 1927. She was to be 26,943 grt with two propellers. White Star Line ordered another new ship, to be named *Oceanic*, in 1928.

Oceanic was originally to be a 60,000-grt liner, and 304m (1,000ft) long. White Star ordered the ship built with a diesel-electric powerplant. The proposal was for forty diesel generators, which would power four propellers at a speed of close to 30 knots. But the project suffered many delays.

P&O entered their new ship, *Viceroy of India*, into service in 1929. She had a turbo-electric powerplant driving two propellers. Built for the Indian mail route, she was also designed to be able to undertake leisure cruises. Considerably smaller than the ships built for the premier transatlantic service, at only 19,648 grt, she nonetheless proved the capability of turbo-electric for P&O.

In Germany, Norddeutscher Lloyd were building cutting edge ships of their own, with *Bremen* and *Europa* entering service in 1929. Both ships were built with a bulbous bow, a protruding structure at the waterline of the bow, which helped to reduce wave resistance. A bulbous bow had been fitted on the USS *Delaware* as early as 1910 but had not yet really caught on in passenger shipping.

In addition to their revolutionary hull design, *Bremen* and *Europa* were also distinctive in that they carried a seaplane aboard for the mails. This aircraft was launched by a catapult on the upper deck and would be loaded with urgent mails and launched several hours before the ships arrived into port.

Both *Bremen* and *Europa* benefitted from modifications made to the Parsons turbine design that gave them greater speed and efficiency. They were fitted with four propellers, driven by a high-pressure, medium-pressure, low-pressure and reverse turbine. On her maiden voyage, *Bremen* captured the Blue Riband with a time of four days, seventeen hours and forty-two minutes. When *Europa* entered service the following year she shaved thirty-six minutes off *Bremen*'s time, capturing the speed record for herself.

In July 1929 White Star Line put the building of *Oceanic* on hold. Instead, they prioritised the completion of *Britannic*, with the ship entering service in June 1930. Plans for *Oceanic* were eventually permanently shelved, with White Star Line choosing to build a running mate for *Britannic* instead. This new ship was slightly larger than *Britannic* and was named *Georgic*. She was to be the last ship built for the White Star Line.

The good times were already beginning to fade. The stock market crash on 29 October 1929 set in motion a series of events that ultimately led to the Great Depression. A stark drop in passenger numbers and cargo over the next few years would lead to financial strain for most of the world's shipping companies.

As the impacts of the Great Depression started to hurt global economies, shipping lines scrambled to source alternative income streams for their ships. Cruising was one area where many executives pinned their hopes, to varying degrees of success.

The strain of the depression saw a number of smaller, intermediate ships withdrawn from service, while large express liners were pushed into an unusual combination of line voyages and cruise holidays.

To that end, Cunard's *Aquitania* and *Mauretania* were sent cruising, with the latter being repainted white in a futile attempt to try and cool the ship in the hot climates of the Caribbean and South American ports being visited.

The White Star Line also turned to cruising to try and stem the losses incurred during the early 1930s, sending their 34,351-grt *Homeric* on a trip to Iceland, though there were no ports of call. By the following year, the ship was placed on full-time cruising duties.

In 1932 cruising was established in Australia by both P&O and Orient Line. P&O's 22,544-grt *Strathaird* was the first to set off, departing in December for a cruise voyage to Norfolk Island. Orient Line sent their similarly sized ship *Oronsay* on a pleasure voyage, with the two departing within a day of each other.

By 1932, 20 per cent of the world's ships were laid up, unable to operate viably in the financial climate they found themselves in. Despite this, innovations were still being applied on the ships that were just coming into service. The motorship *Victoria*, built for Lloyd Triestino, was one of the first in the world built to the newly agreed SOLAS (1929) safety standards. She was also notable as being the first passenger vessel built with air conditioning. The Carrier air conditioning system was fitted to select first-class areas, making a much more comfortable experience for those passengers.

Another big improvement in passenger comfort was the introduction of stabilisation technology. Since the dawn of the passenger ship, the motion of an ocean voyage had been a noticeable deterrent for many potential travellers. While millions had braved an ocean crossing, days or weeks at sea was a source of dread. Concerns over well-being, both physical and mental, had certainly stunted the growth of the fledgling cruise industry, but it also acted as a deterrent for even the wealthy indulging in non-essential line voyages.

Technology to reduce the motion of a moving vessel was first mooted in 1851, in the way of gyroscopic devices. Several attempts were made to create workable gyroscopes throughout the nineteenth century, however it was French Physicist Léon Foucault who first employed a gyroscope to help demonstrate his theory on the rotation and movement of the earth.

By the 1860s, the technology had been improved, with electricity allowing for continual motion of gyroscopes, giving some hint to the future revolution these devices would bring to ocean travel.

During the nineteenth century, the Royal Navy had experimented with anti-rolling tanks, which utilised baffles, a device designed to manipulate water flow and thus counter the rolling motion within the tanks. This technology brought limited improvements, so designers turned their attention to gyroscopes.

The result was the invention of the anti-rolling gyroscope. Tested aboard the United States naval vessel USS *Worden* in 1908, the first large-scale use of this technology took place aboard the USS *Henderson*.

Twin 25-ton anti-rolling units were built into the ship, which was commissioned in 1917. The gyroscopic system successfully reduced the ship's rolling motion, leading it to be adapted for future vessels.

Shipbuilders worldwide took notice, with several small steamers being fitted with the technology throughout the 1920s. However, it was not until the 1930s that anti-rolling gyroscopes were catapulted into the limelight.

Conte di Savoia was built by the Cantieri Riuniti dell'Adriatico shipyard in Italy. Launched in 1931, the ship featured three anti-rolling gyroscopes in her forward hull. Like USS *Henderson* and her successors, *Conte di Savoia*'s gyroscopes were large, each weighing in excess of 25 tons.

Having been fitted out, the ship's maiden voyage set sail on the last day of November 1932. Immediately those aboard noticed the improvement in rolling motion, which was greatly reduced thanks to her gyroscopes.

Fleet-mate to the Blue Riband holder, *Rex*, *Conte di Savoia* brought much media attention to her owners, the Italia Line, despite being slower. Newspapers, magazines and even the much-respected *Popular Mechanic* marvelled at her stability. Celebrities, dignitaries and high society did too, with many opting to travel on the ship in order to enjoy a smoother crossing with less seasickness.

In December 1930 Cunard had laid the keel for a new ship of their own. Given the build number 534, the ship was to be 310.7m (1,019.4 ft) long. But in December of 1931 the worsening financial crisis caused the work on the new vessel to grind to a halt.

In France, the French Line had laid down the keel for their own new liner in January 1931. Though the financial situation was no better for them, with assistance from the French government the shipyard was able to continue building work. Three years to the day after the stock market crash *Normandie* was launched in front of 200,000 spectators. After her launch she was given her machinery and fit-out.

The completed *Normandie* had a hydrodynamic hull, with a bulbous bow. She was also given a breakwater to deflect waves from the superstructure, and had an overall clean, elegant appearance.

The passenger spaces were opulent and featured the largest room yet put to sea in its 93m-long (300ft) Grand Saloon. Modelled on the Hall of Mirrors at Versailles, this was purposefully extravagant. *Normandie*'s engines were turbo-electric, and were both highly reliable and required less maintenance than traditional steam turbines. She had also been given air conditioning in some of her first-class areas, making her more comfortable than many of the ships that had come before her.

Normandie departed on her maiden voyage on 29 May 1935, to much fanfare, and arrived in New York four days, three hours and fourteen minutes later, winning the speed record from Italia Line's *Rex*. Despite this achievement, *Normandie* was not a financial success, requiring a government subsidy to maintain her service.

Strathaird (1932–61). The beautifully balanced *Strathaird* was the second in the Strath class of liners. This ship inaugurated scheduled cruise voyages from Australia in 1932. (Henderson & Cremer Collection)

Empress of Britain (1906–30). Resplendent in the livery of Canadian Pacific and proudly sporting three large funnels, the *Empress of Britain* was noted for being a highly economical ship to run. (Michael W. Pocock/www.maritimequest.com)

Entertainment on the early ships. Onboard entertainment has changed a lot over the years. In the 1930s, 'push the bottle' was one of the favoured pastimes on long-duration line voyages. (Henderson & Cremer Collection)

Anastasis (1953–2007). Built as *Victoria* for the Lloyd Triestino line, this ship was the first passenger liner to be fitted with air conditioning. She later served with hospital ship operator Mercy Ships. (Peter Knego/ www.midshipcentury.com)

Queen Mary (1936–67). Cunard-White Star's *Queen Mary* entered service in 1936. She held the transatlantic speed record from 1938 to 1952. (Colin Hargreaves)

In Britain, Cunard and White Star Line had both approached the British government for financial assistance. The government agreed on the proviso that the two companies merged. Negotiations began in 1933 and concluded in May 1934. With negotiations completed, the newly formed Cunard-White Star Line were finally able to recommence work on hull 534 in 1934.

The new ship was not revolutionary in terms of hull design, and her interiors followed the now established art deco style. But the ship, which had been christened *Queen Mary* at her launch in September of 1934, would prove to be popular with the travelling public. She was also a fast ship.

Entering service in May 1936 she first captured the Blue Riband in August of that year. *Normandie* made another record-breaking crossing in 1937, before *Queen Mary* once more proved her superior speed in 1938.

In the meantime, Cunard-White Star had commenced building a running mate for *Queen Mary*. Given the build number 552, the ship's keel was laid at the John Brown Shipyard in Clydebank in December 1936.

Cruise holidays found an advocate in Nazi Germany from 1937, with a new division of the German Labour Front established to operate pleasure voyages. Six ships were utilised for recreational cruises, the largest being the 27,288-grt *Robert Ley*, a close sister to the slightly smaller 25,484-grt *Wilhelm Gustloff*.

Travel aboard the Nazi cruise ships was far removed from the cruises being offered in other countries. The fleet were operated by a variety of German shipping companies, and the voyages were strictly monitored by the Nazis, who effectively transformed the cruise holiday into floating propaganda. The cruising operations formed a central part of their Strength Through Joy programme from 1937 until the outbreak of the Second World War.

Elsewhere, cruising continued to evolve during the 1930s, and after the worst effects of the Great Depression had passed, began to hint at the possibility of a profitable new income stream. For example, by 1938, Holland America Line were offering thirty-six different cruise holidays to a variety of destinations, while lines such as P&O, Orient, Cunard and their subsidiaries continued to send more ships on cruise voyages until the outbreak of war.

DID YOU KNOW?
The Blue Riband refers to the accolade for the fastest westbound transatlantic crossing.

8

NOT THEIR INTENDED USE

By 1938 the threat of another global conflict was beginning to cast a shadow over the world.

The escalating tensions in Europe led to the absence of King George VI at the launch of what was then the world's largest passenger ship at the John Brown Shipyard on 27 September 1938.

The new ship was the running mate of *Queen Mary*. Of similar dimensions to the earlier ship, the introduction of *Queen Elizabeth* would allow Cunard-White Star to establish the first ever two-ship, weekly, transatlantic service.

Technological improvements in the years since *Queen Mary's* design was finalised made *Queen Elizabeth* a very different ship. The twelve boilers aboard *Queen Elizabeth* could produce the same amount of steam as twenty-four aboard *Queen Mary*, giving *Queen Elizabeth* a more fuel-efficient powerplant.

The reduction in boilers also allowed Cunard-White Star to reduce the number of funnels the design required, from three aboard *Mary* to two aboard *Elizabeth*. This opened up a large amount of space both on the top deck, but also internally as the newer ship had less internal volume occupied by exhaust flues.

The funnels showed improvements in design, having an internal support structure built inside them, as had been seen on *Normandie*. This meant that the supporting cables used on older ships were not required aboard *Queen Elizabeth*.

The decks also benefitted from a revised ventilation and fan arrangement, with exhaust and intake fans clustered at the base of the funnels. All these advances gave *Queen Elizabeth* a cleaner, less cluttered profile than *Queen Mary*.

Other passenger shipping lines were also experiencing the impacts of tensions in Europe. P&O's globally disbursed fleet were often exposed to foreign conflicts. As such, the line felt the effects of the Spanish Civil War from 1937, interrupting their Iberian Peninsula services.

The line was also impacted by the Abyssinian Crisis, with a significant reduction in cargo carriage due to the risk of aerial bombing in the waters near the Ethiopian Empire, which then extended to the shores of the Red Sea. The ongoing reduction in services led P&O to further pivot to cruising, with several ships completing pleasure voyages during the late 1930s.

When war broke out in September 1939, passenger lines across the globe were faced with significant changes and hardship. The Second World War started slowly with an eight-month period of relative inactivity on the Western Front characterised as the 'Phoney War'. Even so, shipping lines had to plan fleet movements while dealing with actual or potential requisitions of their ships.

Despite the quietness on the Western Front, the seas were a dangerous place. Nazi U-boats started to take a toll on British and Allied shipping early on, and the P&O liners *Rawalpindi* and *Rajputana* were lost while acting as armed merchant cruisers in the first months of the war.

In fact, when *Rawalpindi* encountered two Nazi battlecruisers the captain was reported to have said, 'We'll fight them both, they'll sink us, and that will be that,' before taking his ship into battle. *Rawalpindi* only lasted forty-five minutes as, despite her military conversion, she was greatly outmatched by purpose-built naval vessels.

During the early months of the war, many of the large British and French transatlantic ships were requested to remain in neutral or Allied foreign ports. *Queen Mary* and *Normandie* were both berthed in New York as a result.

Queen Elizabeth remained under fit-out at Clydebank. This process lasted until February 1940, when it was deemed by the Admiralty that the ship could no longer remain in British waters.

The ship was unceremoniously handed over to Cunard-White Star, never having completed her sea trials. A small crew were signed on to the ship, being required to sign articles of the Secrets Act before embarkation. The planned voyage was for a short trip to Southampton, where provisioning would take place, before a longer voyage westbound. However, this was not to be.

The United Kingdom government were aware of the value of *Queen Elizabeth* as a troop carrier. They also knew the value that the Nazis placed on destroying the ship. Suspecting Nazi spies were operational in Clydebank, an elaborate deception was planned that included docking plans for Southampton being drawn up and forwarded to the shipbuilder.

The ship departed Scotland early on 2 March 1940 having received sealed orders relating to its course, to be opened once at sea. Captain Townley opened the orders, which revealed the destination as New York.

Thus, the career of the world's largest passenger ship, a title that *Queen Elizabeth* would hold until 1996, commenced in dramatic fashion, with no passengers aboard. The untried engines broke in well, allowing *Queen Elizabeth* to make a speedy transit of the Atlantic, arriving unannounced in New York on 7 March.

As the war started to intensify, so did the dangers of working at sea. The newest Union Castle liner at the outbreak of the war was the 27,002-grt *Capetown Castle*, built at Harland and Wolff.

Mauretania (1939–65). Like her namesake, the second *Mauretania* was built in England, however that's where the similarities ended. This ship was larger and sported twin funnels. She ran as a troop ship during the Second World War. (Henderson & Cremer Collection)

Queen Elizabeth (1940–72). Holding the title of world's largest passenger ship from her launch until 1996, *Queen Elizabeth* had a daunting start to her career, with her maiden voyage in 1940 being made in secrecy. (Henderson & Cremer Collection)

Queen Mary (1936–67). The 1940 arrival of *Queen Mary* in Sydney was a spectacle. Despite the worsening global war, and the ship's greyed-out colour scheme, thousands of Australians took time out to view the massive liner. (Henderson & Cremer Collection)

Empress of Britain (1931–40). In an age before azipods, or bow and stern thrusters, ocean liners of old were tricky to manoeuvre in close quarters. *Empress of Britain* can be seen here in the company of five tugboats. She was lost during the Second World War. (Bill Miller Collection)

Orama (1924–40). Whether migrating to a new land, or heading off to war, sailing day was an emotional experience for many. Peacetime voyages were characterised by the tradition of streamer throwing as the ship left the pier. (Henderson & Cremer Collection)

Like most of the Union Castle steamers, the ship was requisitioned for use as a troop transport. Being British flagged meant the liners would serve the British Admiralty, with *Capetown Castle* being called into service in February 1940.

Refitted to carry thousands more troops than her peacetime passenger capacity, the ship was involved in a narrow escape later that year when several bombs were dropped by a low-flying aircraft, missing the ship by mere metres.

Cunard-White Star's *Mauretania* and *Queen Mary* were both requisitioned and sent to Sydney for trooping conversion. Both ships left New York within a day of each other but were sent to Australia via differing routes.

Queen Mary's arrival in Sydney brought intense public interest. Australian newspapers regularly covered the exploits of transatlantic ships, including *Queen Mary*'s record-breaking peacetime crossings.

The Sydney Harbour ferries ran special services with crowds of spectators aboard, eager to catch a glimpse of the giant ocean liner anchored in Sydney Harbour. *Queen Mary* was already painted in wartime grey, but a subsequent refit carried out by the Cockatoo Dry Dock Co. reworked her on-board spaces, allowing the ship to carry upwards of 10,000 troops.

Mauretania received a similar refurbishment, while *Queen Elizabeth* was activated in November 1940 and sent to Singapore for her refit. These three transatlantic liners were joined by ships of numerous other fleets including P&O, Orient Line, New Zealand Shipping Company and Bibby Line to transfer Australian troops, initially to the Middle East.

Passenger liners were also used to transport New Zealand troops, with the Canadian Pacific Liners *Empress of Britain*, *Empress of Canada* and *Empress of Japan* being utilised on services to Scotland.

In peacetime, New Zealand saw regular visits by ships from the Shaw Savill Line. After the outbreak of war some of these vessels remained on their commercial cargo routes, albeit with a reduced frequency.

One such example was the *Dominion Monarch*. Originally built as a 27,155-grt combination liner, the ship had limited passenger capacity in peacetime, offering accommodation to just 525 first-class passengers. Initially the ship was kept operational in a commercial role, however as the war worsened, she was requisitioned.

Following its wartime conversation, the ship's vast storage spaces were retrofitted, allowing her to transport over 3,500 troops, and the ship ran on the Australian and South African trooping service.

Multiple other passenger ships were converted into troop carriers, with the Middle East and Egypt being an early staging point. The Union of South Africa utilised British-flagged ships as troop transports, including many vessels from the Union Castle Line. *Mauretania* would ultimately serve on the Durban trooping service, joined by the Dutch liner *Nieuw Amsterdam*, which had been requisitioned by the British after the Netherlands were invaded by the Nazis.

As during the First World War, ships were still the most effective way to move people and goods over distances. As such, shipping lines were still required to undertake passenger and cargo services, despite the dangers present.

Orient Line's *Orontes* was required to undertake British government mail services as well as trooping services during 1940. *Orama* and *Ormonde*, on the other hand, were specifically requisitioned for passenger services, running as 'requisitioned liners', while the *Orion* was used as a floating depot ship off Norway in aid of the Allied war effort there.

The evacuation of Europe in 1940 saw some of the most horrendous passenger ship losses of the war, as well as some narrow escapes. On 17 June the Cunard-White Star *Lancastria* was bombed and sunk, with a tremendous loss of life.

The ship was evacuating people from France as the Nazis advanced. It was so hurriedly loaded and carrying so many more people than its design allowed that the total number of people lost is unknown, but it is estimated to be upwards of 4,000.

That same day, the Orient Liner *Oronsay* was nearly lost off the coast of Saint-Nazaire, when the vessel was attacked during evacuation efforts. Remarkably, despite ordnance targeting the bridge and chartroom, the ship was able to escape.

Passenger ships were also employed in the evacuation of children, with the transatlantic Britain to Canada service being one of the more frequent routes. Orient liners including *Oronsay* were employed by the Children Overseas Reception Scheme, with their children's playrooms and facilities briefly reactivated for the purpose.

Ormonde (1917–52). *Ormonde* entered service as a troop ship during the First World War and went on to serve king and country once again during the Second World War. She sailed with Orient Line until 1952. (Henderson & Cremer Collection)

Oronsay (1925–42). *Oronsay* was sunk in the Atlantic Ocean in October 1942 following an encounter with the Italian submarine *Archimede*. (Henderson & Cremer Collection)

Strathallan (1937–42). One of P&O's Strath-sisters, *Strathallan* was built for the long-duration Australian run. She was sunk during the Second World War in the North African campaign. (Henderson & Cremer Collection)

Viceroy of India (1929–42). Another iconic P&O liner lost during the Second World War, *Viceroy of India* was originally built for Britain to India line voyages. (Henderson & Cremer Collection)

Cathay (1925–42). While transporting Allied troops in North Africa in 1942, *Cathay* was bombed and sunk by Nazi bombers. (Henderson & Cremer Collection)

Narkunda (1920–42). Having successfully transported Allied troops to North Africa, *Narkunda* was bombed by Nazi aircraft and later sunk. (Henderson & Cremer Collection)

Empress of Russia (1913–45). *Empress of Russia* served as an armed merchant cruiser and a troop carrier during the First World War. During the Second World War she was called into service once again, but during a refit in 1945 she was destroyed by fire. (Michael W. Pocock/ www.maritimequest.com)

Georgic (1932–56). The last ship built for the White Star Line, *Georgic* was bombed while operating for the Allies in the Gulf of Suez. The ship was later salvaged and returned to service. (George Frame)

Otranto (1925–57). *Otranto* served as both troop carrier and landing assault ship during the Second World War. Allied passenger ships regularly carried far more troops during wartime than their normal passenger capacity. (Henderson & Cremer Collection)

The United States was attacked by the Empire of Japan at Pearl Harbor on 7 December 1941. The subsequent entrance of America into the war changed the dynamics for passenger liners. The Matson Line's *Monterey* was requisitioned by the US government that same month, and on 16 December the ship set out to Pearl Harbor with over 3,300 troops.

Monterey was joined by fellow Matson Line ships *Mariposa* and *Lurline*, running trooping services in the Pacific Ocean, often calling at Hawaii, Suva and Australia. Like the fast British express liners, these American ships would often sail without escorts, relying on their speed to outrun enemy shipping.

With America now at war with Nazi Germany, the US Navy seized the French Line's *Normandie* in December 1941 and planned to convert it into a troop carrier. Her addition to the war effort would have given the Allies another very large troop transport, which would have significantly assisted the war effort.

Renamed *Lafayette*, the vessel was under conversion in New York when a serious fire broke out aboard, caused by stray sparks from a welder's torch. The ship's internal fire suppression system had been deactivated during the conversion work, and the flames quickly engulfed the ship. New York fireboats attended the blaze, pouring a deluge of water into the ship and causing the former French flagship to capsize in the harbour.

In 1942, the world's two largest troop carriers, *Queen Mary* and *Queen Elizabeth*, were repositioned to the Atlantic Ocean. Having received a further refurbishment, their troop-carrying capacity was enhanced. Both ships were now able to carry more than 15,000 troops, with the *Queen Mary* holding the record for the most people ever carried on a passenger ship, 16,683 in a single crossing.

During the 1942 evacuation of Singapore forty-five ships were utilised, including passenger ships, cargo ships and naval vessels. One of the ships involved was the British River Ship *Kung Wo*, which was targeted by the Japanese but was able to escape. The former passenger ship would later be requisitioned for use as a minelayer but was lost off the coast of Indonesia.

The Empire of Japan had one of the largest merchant navies in the world prior to the Second World War, with roughly 2,100 ships in 1936. With their declaration of war in the Pacific, many of the Japanese-flagged passenger vessels were requisitioned for military purposes. These ships were used as troop carriers as well as to transport cargo and military supplies.

Numerous Japanese passenger liners and cargo ships were also used to transport prisoners of war, in horrendous conditions. Fraught with overcrowding and with little in the way of basic provisions, these ships became known as 'Hell Ships' by the Allies, and often saw prisoners held below decks, in space originally designed as cargo holds.

Tragically, a number of 'Hell Ships', full of Allied prisoners of war, were sunk by the Allies during aerial raids. A total of seventeen such losses were recorded from 1942 until the Japanese surrender.

Many Allied passenger ships were also used in the North African campaign. The Union Castle Line was well represented here, with *Warwick Castle*, *Durban Castle*, *Llangibby Castle*, *Capetown Castle* and *Athlone Castle* among those used. They were joined by P&O liners in North Africa, however the company fared poorly, losing *Strathallan*, *Viceroy of India*, *Cathay*, *Narkunda* and *Ettick* during the campaign.

When the Allies advanced on Nazi Germany, the former German liner *Europa* was captured. She had been berthed at Bremerhaven for much of the war. Painted in a dazzle scheme, reminiscent of First World War troop ships, she had been earmarked for use in the planned Nazi invasion of Britain. The ship was activated as the USS *Europa* and pushed into US trooping service.

Wilhelm Gustloff, the Nazi cruise ship, was sunk by Soviet submarine *S-13* while participating in operation Hannibal, the evacuation of civilians and troops from East Prussia and the Baltic. The ship was believed to be carrying more than 10,500 people, with a death toll of more than 9,000.

When hostilities formally ended in September 1945, passenger ships had once again had a huge impact. Their troop-carrying capacity had enabled the mass transportation of thousands of people across the globe, making significant turning points such as the D-Day landings possible.

The British Prime Minister praised the troop ships, in particular *Queen Mary* and *Queen Elizabeth*. As the world's largest passenger ships, they had become unquestionably valuable as troop carriers. The transatlantic shuttle service offered in the lead-up to the D-Day landings meant that the majority of American and Canadian troops involved had crossed the Atlantic aboard the Queens.

Of this service, Churchill wrote, 'Built for the arts of peace and to link the Old World with the New, the Queens challenged the fury of Hitlerism in the Battle of the Atlantic. Without their aid the day of final victory must unquestionably have been postponed.'

Passenger shipping losses had been numerous during the war. Remarkably many of the world's most iconic ships had survived; however, many other passenger ships had been lost.

The Japanese lines, including Nippon Yusen Kaisha K.K., had lost large percentages of their fleets, and many ships that survived the war were seized as war reparations.

Bremen was destroyed by fire in 1942, while *Rex* was bombed in 1944 and lost. *Conte di Savoia* was damaged the previous year. Although restored, she would never sail commercially again. Likewise, *Normandie* would never see passenger service again, having been too badly damaged by fire, and was broken up.

The White Star liner *Georgic* was heavily damaged by fire in the Gulf of Suez, but remarkably was rebuilt and returned to service, first as a troop carrier and later as an immigrant ship. *Europa* ended up joining the French Line as reparations for the *Normandie*, and despite a severe collision with the liner *Paris* she was restored and entered service as *Liberté*. Orient Line was left with just four ships following the war, while Canadian Pacific lost twelve vessels.

Repatriation services were run for the remainder of 1945 and well into 1946 – with the service utilising some of the most famous ships in the world. They also operated a robust global war bride service, with ships from a variety of Allied lines helping to reunite newly married couples.

With the hostilities over, it was now time to refurbish and rebuild, to restore passenger ships to their intended purpose of peacetime crossings and cruises.

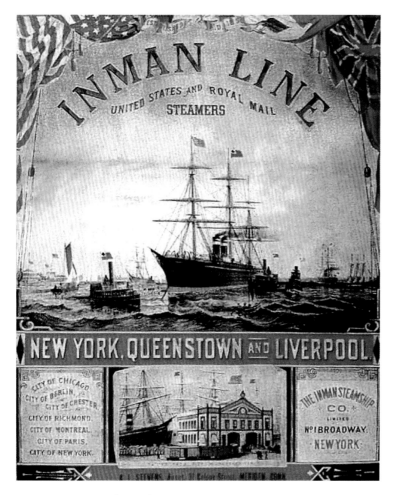

Inman Line poster (c.1887). The Inman Line ran steamships between New York, Queenstown (now Cobh) and Liverpool between 1857 and 1893. In 1886 the company was purchased by International Navigation Co. In 1893 the Inman Line ships were all transferred to the American Line and reflagged in the USA. (Bill Miller Collection)

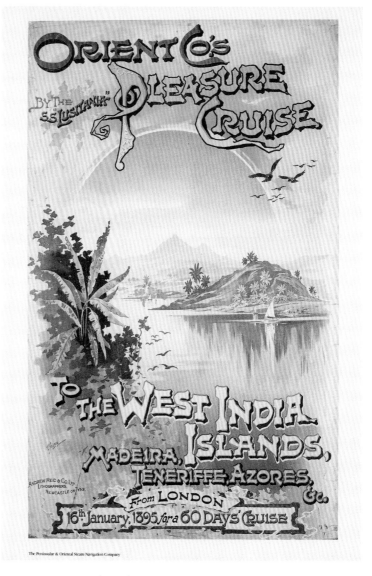

Orient Line poster (1894). Orient Line was one of the first shipping lines to operate dedicated cruise itineraries. (Henderson & Cremer Collection)

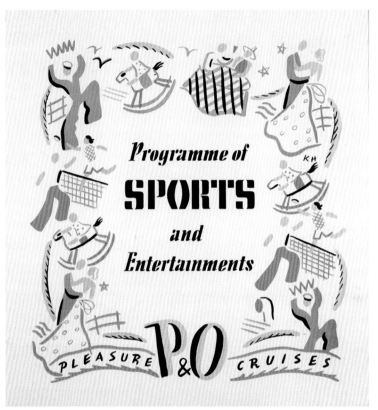

Clockwise from top left: P&O Pleasure Cruises poster (1909). In 1909 P&O offered cruises on both *Vectis* and *Malwa*. (Henderson & Cremer Collection); *Strathmore* programme of sports and entertainments (1930s). On early cruises and line voyages, passengers had to come up with their own entertainment, though the purser's office would often support them by printing programmes. (Henderson & Cremer Collection); Bell of *Oronsay* (1951–75). *Oronsay* was the second Orient Line ship built after the Second World War and the third last built for the line. *Oronsay* was notable for inaugurating Orient Line's transpacific voyages as well as bringing many immigrants to Australia under the Assisted Passage Scheme. (Frame & Cross)

Britannic (1930–61). One of the last ships built for the White Star Line, *Britannic* had a diesel powerplant and was the second largest motorship in the world when built. (Henderson & Cremer Collection)

Parthia (1948–69). Cunard's combination liners *Parthia* and *Media* had a small passenger complement, all travelling in first class. They were popular with celebrities, including Katharine Hepburn. (Henderson & Cremer Collection)

French Line C.G.T.

SOUTHAMPTON TO NEW YORK
EXPRESS LUXURY SERVICE
"ILE DE FRANCE" "NORMANDIE"
ENQUIRE WITHIN

Clockwise from top left: *Queen Mary* (1936–67). While quite traditional in her overall design, *Queen Mary* was the first Cunard express liner to feature a cruiser stern. (Colin Hargreaves); French Line poster (*c.*1935–39). *Normandie* was the biggest and fastest ship when she entered service in 1935 and in addition to sailing from France also offered services to Southampton, England. (Bill Miller Collection); *Britanis* (1932–2000). Refurbished many times during her career, *Britanis* maintained a cruising schedule until 2000, even though she was superseded by many new ships in the busy Florida cruise market. (Peter Knego/www.midshipcentury.com)

Oriana (1960–86). The last ship built for the Orient Line, *Oriana* was the ultimate expression of Orient Line's prevailing philosophy of bridge-amidships design. (Henderson & Cremer Collection)

Pacific Princess (1971–2013). *Pacific Princess* catapulted cruising into American living rooms when she appeared as the location for the television series *The Love Boat*. (Peter Knego/www.midshipcentury.com)

Wooden lifeboat. Lifeboats were initially open-topped wooden boats that were powered by oars. Evacuating by lifeboat was a scary prospect, as lifeboats were not suited for rough seas and bad weather. (Frame & Cross)

Modern lifeboat. Today's lifeboats are motorised and often enclosed, offering safety improvements over the early types. Additionally, they are fitted with radar and radio, allowing the crew to communicate their position, which makes boats easier to track. (Frame & Cross)

Seabourn Odyssey (2009–). *Seabourn Odyssey* features all-suite accommodation, marking it as a luxury cruise offering. There are numerous other inclusions, including dining at all four restaurants. (Frame & Cross)

Queen Elizabeth (2010–). World cruising has come a long way since the first attempts were made, with segments now available to suit most budgets, visiting many countries of the world. (Frame & Cross)

Oriana (1995–). P&O's *Oriana* was built to offer full-time cruising in the British market and was designed with the largest, unobstructed, West End-style theatre at sea when the ship entered service. (Frame & Cross)

Shieldhall (1955–). *Shieldhall* is Britain's largest working steamship, and is powered by reciprocating engines. The preservation of this vessel gives modern-day visitors a glimpse into technology that once dominated passenger shipping. (Frame & Cross)

Flags on the mast. Ships' masts still play an important role today, being a platform for navigation aids, communication, and the hoisting of flags. Common flags flown from the mast include that of the nation of registry, the company flag, and the nation that the ship is visiting. Signal flags indicate the status and intentions of a ship. (Frame & Cross)

Oriana (1995–). Anchored off Guernsey during a 2018 cruise, *Oriana*'s ducktail was added in 2011 in an attempt to reduce the vibrations from cavitation that had plagued the ship since she was introduced. (Frame & Cross)

Tugboat, Wellington. Though much more common in the years prior to the advent of bow thrusters, stern thrusters and azipods, tugboats are still in use around the world. Tugs are called upon to help guide passenger ships when undertaking manoeuvres in port. (Frame & Cross)

Jadrolinija Ferries, Split. The Jadrolinija ferries operate in the Adriatic, offering both domestic and international routes. (Frame & Cross)

Queen Elizabeth 2 (1969–2008). *QE2*'s dual-purpose design blended the seakeeping qualities of an ocean liner with the amenities of a cruise ship. This allowed *QE2* to complete over thirty-nine years of regular transatlantic crossings and cruises. (Frame & Cross)

Anthem of the Seas (2015–) passes *Queen Victoria* (2007–). Superstructures have grown since the first unified deckhouse aboard *Oceanic* in 1871, to tower many stories above the hull in modern cruise ships. (Frame & Cross)

Voyager of the Seas (1999–). With twin azipods and four bow thrusters, *Voyager of the Seas* can usually depart from port without the aid of tugboats. (Frame & Cross)

Tender Boat, *Norwegian Spirit* (1998–). The original ocean liners utilised ferries that were based in the ports that they visited to move passengers and baggage from ship to shore. These days cruise ships carry their own motorised tender boats with them, allowing them to visit a wider range of ports. (Frame & Cross)

Le Lapérouse (2018–). The Ponant Explorer-class ships, including *Le Lapérouse,* feature the Blue Eye Lounge, a lounge with windows under the waterline, allowing guests to view the ocean life around the ship. (Frame & Cross)

Clockwise from top left: Bow of *Pacific Jewel* (1991–2020). Designed by famous architect Renzo Paino, the *Crown Princess* and her sister *Regal Princess* had an exterior profile that was supposed to resemble a dolphin. Renamed *Pacific Jewel* in 2009, the former *Crown Princess*'s bridge was far closer to the tip of the bow than what was typically seen on passenger ships of the past. (Frame & Cross); *Pacific Explorer* (1997–). The second in the Sun-class cruise ships built for Princess Cruises, *Pacific Explorer* started her career as *Dawn Princess*. Today she sails with P&O Australia and was the only Sun-class ship to remain with Carnival Corporation following the COVID-19 pandemic. (Frame & Cross); Stern of *Norwegian Spirit* (1998–). Built in the late 1990s, the refurbished *Norwegian Spirit* benefits from a terraced aft stern that offers plenty of open deck space for passengers to relax, and take in the view. (Frame & Cross); Balcony Cabin, *Pacific Explorer* (1997–). With a heritage dating back to Princess Cruises, the cabins aboard P&O Cruises *Pacific Explorer* resemble the basic design found aboard other Sun-class and Grand-class cruise ships. (Frame & Cross).

Allure of the Seas (2010–). An Oasis-class ship, *Allure of the Seas* is 225,282 gt. The ship has a maximum capacity of 6,780 passengers and 2,200 crew. (Andrew Sassoli-Walker/www.solentphotographer.com)

Borealis (1997–) and *Bolette* (2000–). Originally built as *Rotterdam* and *Amsterdam* for Holland America Line, *Borealis* and *Bolette* were renamed by Fred Olsen Cruise Line when they were purchased in 2020. (Andrew Sassoli-Walker/www.solentphotographer.com)

Marella Discovery (1996–). An all-inclusive cruise ship operating for Marella Cruises/TUI, *Marella Discovery* is their largest vessel. *Marella Discovery* was originally built as *Splendour of the Seas*. (Andrew Sassoli-Walker/www.solentphotographer.com)

Sapphire Princess (2004–). The second Gem-class ship completed for Princess Cruises, *Sapphire Princess* was originally laid down as *Diamond Princess* at Mitsubishi Heavy Industries. After a fire caused construction delays the names of the two ships were swapped, with the original *Sapphire Princess* becoming *Diamond Princess* and vice versa. (Andrew Sassoli-Walker/www.solentphotographer.com)

Volendam (1999–). Ships are uniquely capable of providing additional temporary accommodation in port cities when needed. Examples include *Queen Mary 2* being chartered as an accommodation ship during the Athens Olympics and *Volendam* being chartered in 2022 by the City of Rotterdam to provide accommodation to Ukrainian families. (Andrew Sassoli-Walker/www.solentphotographer.com)

Norwegian Bliss (2018–). At 168,028 gt, *Norwegian Bliss* features an electric go-kart track in addition to laser tag, water slides and a snow room. (Andrew Sassoli-Walker/www.solentphotographer.com)

Top deck of *Coral Princess* (2003–). One of the first ships to feature a pool on board was White Star Line's *Adriatic* (1907). Today most of the larger cruise ships feature multiple pools on board. (Frame & Cross)

Opposite page:
Top: *Scarlet Lady* (2020–). *Scarlet Lady* had a very delayed start to service, with the cruise pause leading to the cancellation of her planned maiden season in 2020. (Andrew Sassoli-Walker/www.solentphotographer.com)
Bottom: *Queen Mary 2* (2004–). The largest ocean liner ever built, *Queen Mary 2* offers regular transatlantic voyages in addition to cruise itineraries including world cruises. (Luke Morrison)

Scenes off Manila (2020). A cluster of cruise ships gather off the coast of Manila, Philippines, during the cruise shut down. Manila was one of few ports that welcomed cruise ships during the early days of the pandemic. (Alison Morton)

9

THE LAST AGE OF THE LINER

In the years immediately following the Second World War, passenger shipping lines focused on the immense task of rebuilding their fleets. The wartime years had brought major losses, however technological advances achieved during the conflict led to a hastened evolution in passenger shipping design.

The rebuilding effort started early, with Orient Line laying down a new ship at the Vickers-Armstrongs yard in September 1945. Named *Orcades*, the 28,164-grt vessel was constructed with a heavy use of welding, considered a stronger and less time-consuming practice when compared to traditional rivets.

Modern arc welding had been invented as far back as 1800, however shipbuilders predominantly utilised riveting techniques up until the Second World War. The use of welding had been instrumental in the development of the Liberty Ship, which helped turn the tides of war in favour of the Allies.

These American-built vessels could be constructed in a fraction of the time of traditionally built ships and employed prefabrication techniques made possible thanks to welding.

Although over 2,700 Liberty Ships were built, welding was a relatively new practice for British shipyards. Thus, *Orcades* was viewed with much interest and some scepticism by the UK shipbuilding community.

By this time, P&O and Orient Line were sharing resources, the former having owned a majority stake in the latter since 1918. As such, the *Orcades* hull design was adapted by P&O for use in their post-war new build, *Himalaya*.

Himalaya was built at the same shipyard as *Orcades*. Despite sharing an almost identical hull design, *Himalaya*'s superstructure was vastly different from her Orient Line cousin. While *Orcades* sported a radical and somewhat unconventional bridge amidships layout, *Himalaya* was much more traditionally balanced.

Himalaya had a traditional mast, rigging and crow's nest, in place of *Orcades*' modern central mast atop the bridge. The internal spaces of both ships also differed, and although *Himalaya* looked boxier, she achieved less internal space for passengers than the *Orcades* design.

Both lines would refine their respective designs for their subsequent builds. Orient Line welcomed *Oronsay* in 1951 and *Orsova* in 1954, while P&O introduced *Chusan* in 1950 before pivoting to an updated, larger design.

Named *Arcadia* and *Iberia*, they both joined the fleet in 1954. *Arcadia* was constructed at the John Brown yard, while *Iberia* was built by Harland and Wolff, and both were designed to take advantage of increased Australian immigration.

In the post-war era, Australia had realised its vulnerability. With many troops overseas fighting in Europe, the nation had come precariously close to invasion from Japan. As such, in the dying days of the war Prime Minister John Curtin began negotiation with his British counterpart, seeking an increase in migrants from the UK in the post-war era.

In a highly publicised 'populate or perish' speech, Curtin highlighted the need to increase the Australian population in order to best defend the nation against future aggressors.

His successor, Joseph 'Ben' Chifley, oversaw the establishment of the Assisted Passage Scheme in 1945. This effectively subsidised the fare for immigrants to a rate of £10 per person. The New Zealand government established its own migration scheme two years later.

The new schemes opened the floodgates for shipping companies to employ their passenger liners on the Australian and New Zealand run. P&O and Orient Line were already well established in the region, as were Shaw Savill, who placed *Dominion Monarch* on the Australian route.

Orcades (1948–73). *Orcades* was one of the first large-scale new-builds following the Second World War. The ship's design was unusual in its central bridge placement. (Henderson & Cremer Collection)

Himalaya (1949–74). The hull of *Himalaya* was of the same general design as that used for *Orcades*, but that is where the similarities of the two designs stopped. (Henderson & Cremer Collection)

On-board shopping. New liners brought with them new amenities. The inclusion of shopping promenades was popularised during the 1930s and remains popular to this day. (Henderson & Cremer Collection)

Orsova (1954–74). *Orsova* was the third in a trio of ships built for Orient Line. As the final version of this design, the vessel featured a prominent swan-neck bow and no mainmast, giving her a modern, futuristic appearance. (Henderson & Cremer Collection)

Chusan (1950–73). *Chusan* was built for P&O's Asian service. Her geared turbines could generate 42,500 shaft horsepower, giving her a top speed of 22 knots. (Henderson & Cremer Collection)

Arcadia (1954–79). A much-loved liner, *Arcadia* was one of the most popular ocean liners on the UK to Australia run. As a liner she could carry 670 first-class and 753 tourist-class passengers, and when cruising 1,350 in a one-class arrangement. (Henderson & Cremer Collection)

Iberia (1954–73). *Iberia* never enjoyed the same adoration as her fleet-mates, being plagued with mechanical issues for much of her career. The ship's service was cut short in the early 1970s and she was scrapped in Taiwan in 1973. (Henderson & Cremer Collection)

Built for the transatlantic, Norwegian America Line introduced their newest ship, *Oslofjord*, in 1949. The ship featured a streamlined forward superstructure and sharply raked bow, with terraced decks starting three quarters aft, giving her a yacht-like appearance. Her first-class accommodation all included en suite, which made the 16,844-grt ship stand out.

The US government agreed to support the building of a fast and large US-flagged express liner. They had identified a weakness during the Second World War when having to lease foreign-flagged ships to undertake their wartime trooping movements, particularly on the Atlantic. This was best illustrated with the use of *Queen Mary* and *Queen Elizabeth* on the G.I. run.

Ordered by the United States Lines with oversight from the US Navy, the new ship was built at the Newport News Shipbuilding Co. Named *United States*, the 53,330-grt ship did not challenge for the title of world's largest. This design consideration was made purposefully to enable her to transit the Panama Canal, which would be essential should she ever be called into military service.

It was her powerplant that would make her a record breaker. Four Westinghouse geared turbines offered 240,000 rated shaft horsepower. This immense power drove four propellers and gave the ship a top speed of over 38 knots, achieved during sea trials.

The design specifications of the ship led to the creation of not only the fastest liner ever conceived, but also one of the safest. Extensive use of fire-retardant materials gave the ship superior fire proofing, while her hull was divided into multiple watertight compartments, giving her a greater ability to withstand water ingress.

Of the ship's capabilities, her designer William Gibbs said, 'You can't set her on fire, you can't sink her and you can't catch her.'

The ship entered service on 4 July 1952 and immediately captured the eastbound transatlantic speed record, besting the *Queen Mary*'s record by ten hours. She subsequently captured the prestigious Blue Riband with an average speed of 34.51 knots – a record that she holds to this day.

In 1952, Shaw Savill commissioned the construction of their new flagship, *Southern Cross*, which was built at the Harland and Wolff shipyard. At 20,204 grt the ship had a revolutionary exterior design and entered service in 1955.

Her funnel was situated towards the aft of the ship, made possible by a novel engine arrangement that enabled exhaust gases to be released further aft than the typical arrangement on contemporary liners.

The funnel position opened the central space on the ship for enlarged public areas, as well as a massive open top deck for passengers to relax on. The ship had so much deck space that the designers were able to include multiple outdoor swimming pools.

The ship was completed as all-tourist class, given her role as an immigration vessel, however much care was taken to ensure the finishes were of a high standard. Shaw Savill went so far as to include en suite bathrooms in some of the best cabins.

The Suez Canal closure in 1956 led to a shift in shipping routes, with most eastbound liners sailing via South Africa. This led to busy scenes in South African ports such as Cape Town, Durban and Port Elizabeth.

The influx of additional ships led to congestion issues, impacting the long-established Union Castle services. South Africa itself was experiencing a post-war immigration boom, as well as a relatively high level of emigration, leading to a surge in demand for Union Castle passenger services.

Queen Elizabeth (1940–72). Resplendent in her civilian livery, *Queen Elizabeth* was the flagship of the Cunard Line. She worked alongside *Queen Mary* on Cunard's two-ship transatlantic express service until 1967. (Henderson & Cremer Collection)

Queen Elizabeth (1940–72). Transatlantic liners were not known for their manoeuvrability in ports, and required multiple tugs to ease the burden of docking. (Henderson & Cremer Collection)

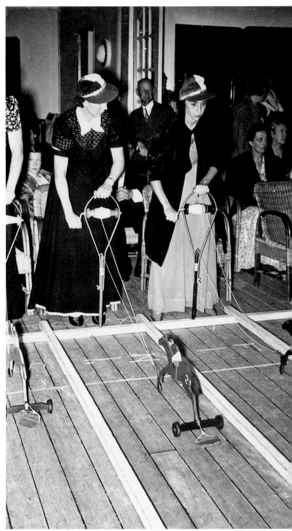

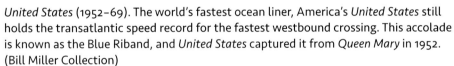

United States (1952–69). The world's fastest ocean liner, America's *United States* still holds the transatlantic speed record for the fastest westbound crossing. This accolade is known as the Blue Riband, and *United States* captured it from *Queen Mary* in 1952. (Bill Miller Collection)

Horse racing. In the age of the ocean liner, shipboard entertainment was very different from a modern-day cruise experience. One of the popular games to play while at sea was 'horse racing'. (Henderson & Cremer Collection)

Quoits. Deck quoits was a popular game throughout the age of the ocean liner and can still be found aboard many cruise ships to this day. (Henderson & Cremer Collection)

Tender service. One of the pitfalls of an ocean liner design was the deep drafts that many of these ships had. This restricted their access to shallow ports that were not accustomed to passenger ships, requiring time-consuming tender services to be undertaken. (Henderson & Cremer Collection)

Norwegian America Line improved on the *Oslofjord* design when, in 1956, they introduced the *Bergensfjord*. At 2,000 grt larger than her fleet-mate, the newer ship featured enhanced on-board amenities, with en suite for all passengers regardless of class.

On the evening of 25 July 1956 the Swedish America liner *Stockholm* collided with the Italia Societa di Navigazione ocean liner *Andrea Doria*. The ships were both sailing off the coast of Nantucket, Massachusetts, in dense fog when the incident occurred, with the *Stockholm* crashing into *Andrea Doria*'s starboard side.

The damage to both vessels was significant. *Stockholm*'s bow was effectively crumpled away, well past the location of the anchors. The damage to *Andrea Doria* was less obvious yet more severe, with a significant list to starboard caused by water entering the starboard ballast tanks, while the port tanks remained empty.

Andrea Doria's severe list would ultimately prove unrecoverable, however before the ship foundered the ship's crew commenced evacuation. The vessel had a ship-wide public address system, allowing the crew to communicate with the passengers, only calling for them to abandon ship when the situation had been fully assessed, and egress paths determined on the heavily listing ship.

However, evacuation was made challenging due to the list, which made the lifeboats very difficult to handle. Fortunately, *Andrea Doria* foundered slowly, allowing enough time for rescue ships to arrive. This included the 43,135-grt *Île de France*, which received the stricken liner's SOS while outbound from New York.

By the time *Andrea Doria* sank, 1,660 passengers and crew had been rescued. Tragically forty-six people perished aboard the Italian ship, and five people lost their lives aboard *Stockholm* resulting in a total human loss of fifty-one.

In the aftermath, an inquiry was established in New York, but it was abruptly curtailed when the two shipping lines reached a settlement agreement that hindered the efforts to formalise findings of fault.

A subsequent US Congressional hearing attributed the *Andrea Doria*'s poor ballasting, the speed at which both ships were travelling while navigating fog, the way radar was used aboard *Stockholm* and the handling of *Andrea Doria*'s helm during the incident as contributing factors to the disaster.

DESIGN ENHANCEMENTS

In 1960, Italia Societa di Navigazione introduced a new vessel with a similar profile to the lost *Andrea Doria*. The *Leonardo da Vinci* was paired with the 1950s era *Cristoforo Colombo* on both transatlantic crossings and cruises.

The new ship was several thousand gross registered tons larger than the vessel she replaced and featured a number of safety improvements over her predecessor. These included upgraded lifeboat davits that could better handle severe listing, as experienced when *Andrea Doria* sank. Additionally, the hull was given improved watertight subdivision with heightened bulkheads.

10

THIS CHANGES EVERYTHING

For decades, the ocean liner had dominated global transportation, in particular travel over long distances. From the northern hemisphere, ocean liners had circled the world taking people, goods and mail to all corners of the globe.

Shipping lines had centuries of good times. Although major global events such as wars and economic crises disrupted shipping, ships remained the only feasible way to achieve large-scale, global movement.

The thought of a new mode of transport toppling the liner was as foreign to people of the 1920s as interstellar travel was to someone in the 1990s. And although individual operators might have struggled or ceased operations, there was plenty of business to ensure that the passenger shipping industry thrived.

Shipping lines' business models relied on three key factors. Firstly, passengers, the majority of which had little alternative but to travel by sea. While airlines such as Qantas and KLM commenced services as early as the 1920s, for the first few decades flying was a novel adventure. An observer in 1930 may have argued that large airships were the way of the future, but the disastrous *Hindenburg* catastrophe, and the Second World War, saw the age of the Zeppelins fade, while the passenger ship sailed on.

Freight remained as the second key contributor to the success of passenger shipping. Passenger ships' giant cargo holds were big moneymakers for shipping lines. Liners of all shapes and sizes had cargo compartments. Looking through archival photographs of liners at the pier, one can't help but notice the buzzing activity of loading and unloading cargo, regardless of the port of call.

Purpose-built cargo ships had existed since the dawn of shipping, however for centuries their operation on main-line passenger routes was no more efficient than utilising a passenger ship's cargo holds for transport. Indeed since 1840, express freight benefitted from steam-powered liner services, with passenger ships often running faster than their purely cargo-carrying counterparts.

Finally, the mail service remained a key moneymaker. Shipping lines continued to be paid for transporting the mails. Express post may have made its way across continents by train, and later propeller-driven aircraft, but most of the world's intercontinental post travelled by sea.

Throughout the nineteenth and the first half of the twentieth centuries, innovation and competition had progressed the evolution of the passenger ship, leading to liners of immense size and speed. Nothing successfully challenged the status quo of the passenger ship's position as a global necessity, until the 1950s.

The first blow came from the sky. Pressurised aircraft started flying in 1940, with Boeing leading the way. The 307 Stratoliner was a derivative of the B-17, and while only a handful were built, they paved the way for pressurisation to change global transport.

Super Constellation. The Lockheed Constellation and later Super Constellation introduced fast, pressurised air travel to the market, which started a gradual shift away from travel by sea during the 1950s. (Frame & Cross)

This made other manufacturers, such as Lockheed and Douglas, take notice and develop their own pressurised airliner platforms. By 1943 the Lockheed Constellation was introduced into service. It was followed by the Douglas DC-6 a few years later.

These aircraft revolutionised air travel. The North Atlantic was a key battle ground with multiple players representing both airlines and shipping lines. The distance of the Atlantic proved an excellent testing ground for the new technology. Travelling by air between Europe and America was far quicker than by ship, with the speed of this connection becoming appealing to those who could afford it.

At this stage, neither the Constellation or DC-6 possessed enough range to offer quick point-to-point flights over long distances. Travelling to and from Australia, Asia and Africa required numerous fuelling stops.

However, this did not stop local airlines from jumping on the revolutionary new technology, with Australia's Qantas, Ansett and TAA all operators of early pressurised piston-driven aircraft.

For its part, Qantas pioneered the Kangaroo Route, a multi-stop journey between Brisbane and London. The Constellation's range and comfort allowed for a quicker journey, with Qantas completing the entire Australia to England route with its own aircraft from 1947 (prior to this Qantas flights from Australia to Singapore connected with flights run by other airlines).

The presence of big, pressurised airliners started to erode the profit margins of shipping lines. While long-distance players such as P&O, Orient Line and Union Castle Line noticed the impact of the airliner, transatlantic lines felt it more keenly.

In 1951 Lockheed introduced the stretched Super Constellation, which improved comfort and the reliability of its already popular plane. Douglas followed suit, with the DC-7 entering service in 1953. Thus, as more airlines took up pressurised transatlantic flights, it was in 1957 that more passengers travelled across the Atlantic by air than by ship.

Just two years before the aeroplane eclipsed the ship as a people transport, another innovation entered the scene, the cargo container.

Containerisation is a foundation of life as we know it today, yet it had the humblest of beginnings. The idea was not new, with ships designed to carry standardised loads entering service as early as the eighteenth century.

Yet it wasn't until 1955 that the first ship we'd recognise today as a container ship was built. The *Clifford J. Rogers* was small by today's standards, but she paved a path that led to the global development of containerised cargo transport.

Clifford J. Rogers was followed months later by a ship that is credited as being the first financially successful container ship. Built by the United States during the Second World War, this vessel started its career as an oil tanker.

The steam-powered ship was a far cry from today's massive container ships. Just 16,460 grt, the 160m-long vessel was modified in 1955 and renamed *Ideal-X*. She successfully carried just shy of sixty containers between New Jersey and Texas, proving the efficiency of this new mode of transport.

Within a decade, Australia's *Kooringa* introduced cellular containerisation. This allowed for the simultaneous loading and unloading of cargo, giving the ship a remarkable thirty-six hours turnaround time.

The efficacy of containerised cargo transport was a massive blow to passenger shipping lines. Containers were easier to load and unload, provided greater flexibility and improved protection of the cargo inside. Furthermore, they were interchangeable across a developing network of containerised trucking, rail and sea, though in the early years a plethora of non-compatible standards formed.

Meanwhile, on the passenger front, things were looking grim for the big lines. The revolutionary de Havilland Comet had shown the benefits of jet power as early as the 1940s, and by 1957 Boeing was ready to unleash its latest innovation, the model 707.

The 707 revolutionised the way people travelled, first across the Atlantic and then around the world. Pan American was the first to introduce 707 services, flying their inaugural transatlantic flight on 26 October 1958.

The 707 was faster and quieter than the piston-engine airliners it replaced. It flew higher, with a maximum ceiling of 41,000ft, meaning it offered a smoother ride well above most weather systems. It was also larger, increasing the capacity and offering improved economies of scale for airliner operators.

An improvement in price competitiveness came the following year when Douglas introduced the DC-8. Similar in appearance to the 707, this airliner was purchased by both Delta and United, the latter of which also flew the shorter Boeing 720. American Airlines, TWA, Braniff, Continental and Northwest would all go on to fly 707s, making jet services increasingly accessible for travellers in the United States.

A regular question on the minds of transatlantic travellers became: Why spend days travelling by ship when I can cross the Atlantic in a matter of hours by air?

This question almost always ended in favour of flying, particularly for the wealthier passenger. It became even easier to justify the cost of an air ticket in winter, when rough Atlantic crossings had made sea travel unappealing for decades.

The result was a sustained decline in demand for passenger line voyages, with the North Atlantic route hardest hit in those early years.

As shipping finances became strained, unrest broke out among dock workers, leading to strikes on both sides of the Atlantic. On several occasions through the late 1950s and '60s, the situation became severe.

In New York, striking tugboat workers and longshoremen led to remarkable sights at the historic finger piers involving the *Queen Mary* and *Queen Elizabeth,* still the largest express liners afloat.

These ships were not easy to manoeuvre, introduced long before bow thrusters or rotating azipods (steerable propulsion systems) became the norm. Manoeuvrability in close quarters relied on tugboat assistance, but not on these occasions. With tugs unavailable, the ships were forced to dock unaided, something that showed the skill of their officers and crew and gained accolades in the media.

Though the disruption of the jet was certainly a turning point for shipping lines, not all lines were taken by surprise. Holland America Line had seen the writing on the wall earlier than most. As the line's fleet experienced increasing competition from the air, they built new tonnage to turn the tides of fortune.

This shift in strategy culminated with *Rotterdam*, built in 1959 at the Rotterdam Drydocks Co. shipyard. Created to be able to undertake traditional Netherlands to America line voyages, *Rotterdam* wowed passengers with a radical new design that hinted at an alternative cruising use.

With *Rotterdam*, Holland America had developed a dual-purpose liner. Built strong, fast, and stable enough to undertake regular scheduled crossings, the design also incorporated an array of cruise-friendly elements.

Rio Negro (2008–). Containerisation changed the way goods were moved around the globe and saw cargo carriage move from ocean liners to fleets of container ships. (Frame & Cross)

Rotterdam (1959–2000). *Rotterdam* was built as a dual-purpose liner. Her cruise-friendly design traits allowed the ship to enjoy a long career. (Rob Lightbody)

Rotterdam (1959–2000). During the age of the ocean liner, it was common to see gangways branded for the shipping line and/or the name of the ship. This is replicated at the Rotterdam Hotel. (Rob Lightbody)

Rotterdam (1959–2000). Dutch interior designer Van Tienhoven was responsible for the overall design architecture aboard the *Rotterdam*. Many of the original interior spaces have been lovingly restored aboard the ship. (Rob Lightbody)

The ship was taller, sleeker, and more streamlined than her contemporaries and sported twin thin funnels. She was a two-class ship, with Holland America realising there was little market for third class in the age of increasingly affordable air travel.

Importantly, she could sail as a single-class ship when cruising, and her design incorporated swimming pools, open-air entertainment spaces and lots of windows, allowing travellers to connect with the surrounds of their cruise destinations. The ship entered service in 1959 on the transatlantic route, however, increasingly the liner was sent on cruises, and became a dedicated cruise ship in the 1970s.

While the Atlantic was the first region to see ocean liner dominance falter, the jet had a domino effect globally. Qantas was the first non-US carrier to run Boeing 707 services, with its first jet-powered flight taking off in 1959.

This move started to slowly erode the Australian passenger services of the various lines servicing this route, including P&O, Orient Line and Shaw Savill. However, the vast distances between Europe and Australia, as well as the Australian government's immigration policy, offered a reprieve for the ocean liner on this route.

The Assisted Passage Scheme provided shipping lines with an opportunity to capitalise at a time when operational margins were lean in most parts of the world. Orient Line ran three premier liners on the route, *Orcades*, *Oronsay* and *Orsova*, while the larger P&O utilised a variety of ships including *Arcadia*, *Iberia* and *Chusan*.

As passenger numbers grew during the 1950s, jet services were unable to keep pace. As revolutionary as jet flights were, these early airliners had limited capacity. Furthermore, their range was restricted by fuel-hungry turbojets, which led to high fares and multiple stops on the journey to Australia.

P&O, Orient Line and Shaw Savill were all confident enough with the Assisted Passage business model that they each committed to a new ocean liner.

Built at Vickers-Armstrongs, the 41,900-grt *Oriana* entered service for Orient Line in 1960. She became the fastest ship to operate on the Australian run, with a top speed of 30 knots. She was followed a year later by P&O's *Canberra*. Built at the

Harland & Wolff shipyard, *Canberra* was the larger of the two, clocking in at 45,270 grt.

Oriana and *Canberra* were custom-built for the Australian service, with a tourist-class capacity of around 1,500 and 1,600 respectively. Other design features hinted at their Australian connection, with large open decks, air conditioning and swimming pools being important aspects of a long-duration equatorial crossing.

But the new ships were not enough to counter the appeal of the jet. In 1961, Orient Line was merged into the P&O passenger fleet, becoming P&O-Orient.

Shaw Savill built *Northern Star*, a 24,731-grt ship with a similar profile to their earlier *Southern Cross*. *Northern Star* was built to undertake round-world line voyages to South Africa, Australia and New Zealand and could accommodate around 1,400 passengers.

South African Airways (SAA) also acquired jet airliners in the 1960s, a move that started to put pressure on the largest passenger shipping operator in the region, Union Castle Line.

A few years earlier, Safmarine had been established as a South African bulk freight line. Services commenced with a small fleet of converted Victory Ships, surplus from the US wartime effort. The business continued to grow, introducing larger steam-powered and later diesel ships. Safmarine's focus on containerised cargo put pressure on the neighbouring Union Castle Line, which had historically relied on both passenger and cargo revenues.

Union Castle was British managed and their large liner fleet was registered in the United Kingdom. However, as South Africa increasingly pushed to independently control their international trade, a deal was struck that saw Union Castle ships transferred to the South African-owned Safmarine.

These included the 1961-built *Transvaal Castle*, and the 1947-era *Pretoria Castle*. While *Pretoria Castle* was a vintage, pre-jet liner, the *Transvaal Castle* was not. Nonetheless, the ship was built as a true ocean liner, specifically developed for the Southampton to Durban run.

Yet despite the traditional routing, the ship's design included several innovative features. Notably the John Brown-ship was among the first British liners to feature a bulbous bow, which aided in fuel efficiency and stability. Additionally, her bow flaring was more pronounced than what had been seen on earlier Union Castle ships.

The highly streamlined superstructure was eye-catching and hid another fascinating aspect of this ship, she was one class. Union Castle branded the vessel as a 'hotel ship', a forward-thinking move at the time and one of the reasons why the ship was sought by Safmarine.

Renamed S.A. *Vaal* and S.A. *Oranje*, the two ships were an odd pairing of modernity and tradition. They continued to be operated by Union Castle Line on a charter arrangement. Yet their South African ownership saw them soar in popularity during the 1960s.

Back on the Atlantic, the situation had deteriorated. With growing losses, many shipping lines started to reduce their fleets, laying up surplus tonnage.

Despite airliners eroding passenger ships' market share globally, there were several shipping lines that took advantage of the excess of retiring ocean liners to capitalise on niche-market voyages. The Greek-owned Chandris was one such line.

Formed in 1960 to operate line voyages between Europe and Australia, its founder Anthony Chandris set out to take advantage of the Australian government's Assisted Passage Scheme, and in the process develop what was hoped to be a sustainable liner service, linking the two continents.

The line's first ship, *Patris*, was acquired from the Union Castle Line. The vessel commenced service nine years earlier as the *Bloemfontein Castle*. Understanding the fundamental differences between the traditional Cape-bound line voyages and immigration services to Australia, Chandris invested in reconfiguring the ship for its new role, increasing its passenger capacity and enhancing the interior spaces for the longer-duration Australian voyages.

Patris remained on the Australian route into the 1970s, and the line's approach of purchasing and refurbishing ageing tonnage saw them quickly expand, taking on the 1932-built *Lurline*, renaming her *Ellinis*, as well as acquiring the *Regina*, a ship that had a background as a US Army transport.

In 1964, Chandris made its boldest acquisition yet when it purchased the 220.3m (723ft) long ocean liner *America*. Built for the United States Lines, the ship had been paired with the larger and faster *United States* for the transatlantic express service. *America* was given an extensive refurbishment, emerging as the newly renamed *Australis*.

The refurbishment work increased the ship's passenger capacity, with several hundred new cabins added to the deck plans. The ship would become one of the last to operate on Australian line voyages.

The 1966 Seamen's Strike in the United Kingdom did passenger ships no favours, with British-based vessels stranded for forty-five days. This gave many remaining seagoing passengers their first opportunity to sample air travel.

Ocean-going line voyages were further disrupted in 1967 when the Arab-Israeli war led to the closure of the Suez Canal. Container ships diverted to elongated routes around the Cape of Good Hope, but the impact was most severely felt by passenger steamers and combination liners.

When the Boeing 747 took to the skies in 1969, it delivered one of two unrecoverable blows to the remaining global passenger shipping services.

The 747 first flew commercially with Pan American in 1970, however unlike its single-aisle counterparts, the jumbo jet was massive. Boeing's decision to build a wide-body ushered in the age of high-capacity airliners. Airlines rushed to acquire the Boeing jet, and its swift introduction into service made air travel far more accessible to the masses.

The situation was exacerbated by both Douglas and Lockheed introducing wide-body airliners of their own. The Douglas DC-10 entered service in 1971, while the Lockheed L-1011 TriStar joined airline fleets a year later.

The second unrecoverable blow for ocean liners was the standardisation of container shipping. This started to accelerate during the 1970s. For the first decades of containerised freight services, a variety of standards had been developed. Rival freight companies had built an array of container sizes and coupling systems.

The International Organisation for Standards (ISO) created several standards, beginning in the late 1960s and culminating in the '70s. These covered dimensions, volume, coupling and identification markings.

These same standards were implemented by sea, rail and road operators, creating a truly integrated system. Their integration globally would forever change freight shipping and directly led to the modern, globalised economy we have today.

In spite of the changing landscape, some shipping lines had built three-class ocean liners during the 1960s, which, unsurprisingly, were haemorrhaging financially by the turn of the decade. Italia Societa di Navigazione was one such organisation, with their *Michelangelo* and *Raffaello* both entering service in 1965.

DID YOU KNOW?

P&O's passenger shipping division was known as P&O-Orient in 1961–66 following the merger of the P&O and Orient Line fleets. As the P&O acronym means Peninsular and Oriental, the full name of the line at that time was a somewhat repetitive Peninsular and Oriental – Orient.

Oriana (1960–86). *Oriana* featured multiple levels of open promenade decks at her stern. The ship is seen passing the under-construction Sydney Opera House. (Henderson & Cremer Collection)

Britanis (1932–2000). Built for Matson Lines as *Monterey*, this ship served during the Second World War, initially carrying troops to Hawaii. Returned to her owners, she sailed as *Matsonia* and *Lurline* until the 1970s. The ship then spent the next twenty-eight years operating as *Britanis* for Chandris. (Peter Knego/www.midshipcentury.com)

Opposite page: Clockwise from top left:
Canberra (1961–97). *Canberra* featured a large, curved forward superstructure sporting many large windows, her bridge set about a third the way along her length, and twin thin funnels. (Henderson & Cremer Collection);
Noga (1940–79). A ship of many names, the *America* entered service in 1940 and was involved in wartime duties for the United States as the USS *Westpoint*. The ship later enjoyed an eighteen-year career as a transatlantic liner before sailing as *Australis*, *Italis*, *Noga*, *Alfredos* and *American Star*. She was wrecked in 1994 in the Canary Islands. (Peter Knego/www.midshipcentury.com);
Britanis (1932–2000). When Chandris acquired *Lurline*, they made significant modifications to the ship to best serve their market. Re-emerging as *Britanis*, the ship featured reworked funnels, additional cabins, a new forward cargo derrick and the removal of the original mast. (Peter Knego/www.midshipcentury.com)

Caribe I (1953–2009). Built as the ocean liner *Olympia* for the Greek Line, the ship was used in a cruising role for Commodore Cruise Line during the 1980s and early '90s. The ship would later sail as *Regal Empress* for Regal Cruise Line and Imperial Majesty Cruise Line. (Peter Knego/www.midshipcentury.com)

Fedor Shalyapin (1955–94). Built for Cunard Line as *Ivernia*, the ship was later renamed *Franconia* when she was refurbished for cruising in 1962. Sold in 1973, she would sail as *Fedor Shalyapin* until 1994 under Soviet Union and later Ukrainian control. The ship was scrapped in 2004. (Peter Knego/www. midshipcentury.com)

Margarita L (1960–1977/2005). *Windsor Castle* was once the pride of the Union Castle fleet. She ran on the Cape Town and Durban service until 1977. Sold to Greek interests, the ship was renamed *Margarita L*. Laid up in 1991, she made one final journey under her own steam in 2005, to the breaker's yard. (Peter Knego/www.midshipcentury.com)

France (1962–2003). Built for the French Line, the ship was renowned as the longest passenger liner of all time, a title she held until 2003 when eclipsed by *QM2*. Laid up in 1974 she was later acquired by Norwegian Cruise Line and renamed *Norway*. (Bill Miller Collection)

Their design appeared novel on the outside. They had twin funnels placed in a latticework style that had been crafted in such a way to reduce the likelihood of smoke and soot falling on the aft decks of the ship.

These impressive structures, paired with a single mast as well as a curved forward superstructure, gave both ships a hint of modernity. The pair were placed on the Atlantic route as well as cruises, which increased in frequency the longer the two ships remained active.

By the mid-1970s however, operational costs were high. The ships' three-class layout was difficult to fill, with most passengers disinterested in cruising in lower-class accommodation.

Ultimately, design shortcomings and overheads led to both ships being withdrawn from cruising service in 1975.

A similar fate had befallen the *France* a year earlier. Built for the French Line, the ship had entered service in 1962. *France*, at least, was a two-class liner and the longest passenger ship yet built at the time. Her massive 315m (1,033.4ft) length allowed for a passenger capacity of 2,254.

While the French Line had foresight in the class arrangement, any plans for flexibility in service fell short due to the ship's general design. For instance, her deep draft made arrival and departure challenging for most leisure ports, while the transatlantic nature of her general layout was not ideal for a cruising role.

Issues included a lack of open-air swimming pools (all three of her pools were covered), while the majority of her open decks were exposed to the sun above but sheltered from the wind at the port or starboard side, providing an imperfect combination of hot and view-obstructed deck space.

The 1970s oil crisis played a significant role in hastening the retirement of *France*. This culminated with the end of Trente Glorieuses, bringing a thirty-year period of financial prosperity to an end.

The French government had subsidised *France* throughout her service career. In fact, the government had in many ways encouraged the building of the ship as a showcase to the style, design and prosperity of the nation. Despite attempts to boost the ship's profitability with cruises, in 1974 the subsidies were withdrawn, and the ship made her final crossing as a French liner.

P&O had adapted to the changing environment fairly well, having entered the containerised shipping business in 1965. The organisation invested in ports and bolstered its involvement in ocean-going ferries, which remained profitable on short voyages across the English Channel where the expense of flying was often viewed as exorbitant.

As for their passenger shipping business, P&O faced a similar conundrum to their transatlantic counterparts. Their big liners were built to specifications for long-duration line voyages, with a large portion of small, inside cabins and shared berths. As a result, they began to withdraw most of their older, unprofitable liners.

To that end, P&O ultimately retired *Orcades*, *Oronsay*, *Orsova*, *Himalaya*, *Iberia* and eventually *Arcadia*, all of which were deemed obsolete in the new operational environment. It was hoped the remaining ships could evolve into full-time cruising, with *Oriana* and *Canberra* the main focus for the line.

Their designs featured many cruise-like elements, such as open decks, swimming pools, large picture windows, multiple bars and lounges and air conditioning, the latter critical to keep the ship's interior comfortable during equatorial itineraries.

P&O aspired to break into the emerging American cruise market, and thought *Canberra* was the platform to do it. Unfortunately, the ship's dual-class design and immigration-centric origins fell far short of American expectations. Her inaugural cruising season was so poorly received that the line made plans to retire the ship.

Ocean liners appeared to be fast going extinct, with line after line retiring ships. However, things were about to change. Cruising was on the cusp of its moment in the sun.

A VERY BRIEF HISTORY OF THE FERRY

If you hear the term ferry, you could picture any number of vessels. People in coastal cities may immediately think of relatively large vessels, while many people living near rivers or harbours may picture smaller passenger transports, zipping from shore to shore.

The Encyclopaedia Britannica notes that the earliest-known reference to the ferry stems from the Ancient Greek myth of Charon the Ferryman. In the story, Charon is said to 'ferry souls' of the dead across the River Styx.

This introduces a peculiarity of the term ferry: it can refer to both the act of moving people or goods across a body of water, as well as the vessel that does the ferrying. Thus, the ferry occupies a unique place among passenger ships, in that they transcend the differentiation of boats and ships, as well as the definition of vessel and route.

A ferry can be a boat or ship of any size, used to carry passengers, cargo, vehicles and even trains. Some ferries carry a combination, while others are dedicated to a single type of cargo, be it human or mechanical. A ferry can be very large, the same size as a cruise ship, but they can also be small, the size of a boat. The smallest ferries can seat just a few people.

The earliest ferries were rowboats, used to move people and goods across small waterways, rivers, and canals. The eighteenth century saw engineers attempt to run a steamboat ferry service on America's Delaware River, but it was perhaps the British ferry *Leviathan* that gained the most attention.

Brainchild of engineer Thomas Bouch, the vessel entered service in 1850 and transited the Firth of Forth. It is widely considered the first 'roll on, roll off' (RORO) ferry, as it transported not only passengers but also livestock, goods and importantly wagons, which could be driven on and off the vessel.

By the 1870s ferry design had improved further, with the introduction of a symmetrically ended design. Employed aboard *Suchlet*, the design allowed for a simpler loading and unloading of cargoes thanks to entry ramps on both sides of the ship.

From 1888, Hong Kong established its now-iconic ferry service as the Kowloon Ferry Co. This organised service utilised 100-passenger, multi-storey vessels that were capable of crossing between Hong Kong Island and Kowloon multiple times a day.

Similar services were established in many harbour cities, including Penang, multiple Philippine cities and Sydney, which today is renowned for its iconic Harbour Ferry service.

The first ferry services in Sydney took the form of rowboats, with independent links developed between 1789 and the late 1830s. The growth of Paramatta led to dedicated steamships being deployed from 1832. A decade later ferries were employed on runs across the harbour, and services to Manly commenced from 1855.

These various services ran independently of each other, until the government amalgamated them in 1951. Today the Sydney Ferries operation provides a useful example of how varied ferries can be, as the service utilises numerous types of boats and ships to maintain key transportation links.

Its largest vessels are the 1,150-passenger capacity Freshwater class. With a length of 70.4m (230.97ft), these twin-screw vessels are undoubtedly small ships and have been in operation since 1982. They are juxtaposed with the petite River Cat class. A catamaran design, these ferries are only able to accommodate 200 people. Their 25m (82ft) length blurs the lines that divide boats from ships, and they are dwarfed by the larger Freshwater vessels.

Large-scale ferries are also very common around the world. Perhaps one of the most iconic ferry-served sea routes is the English Channel. Archaeological discoveries suggest the first Channel ferry crossings date back to 1550 BCE, but it wasn't until the 1820s that modern regular crossings began.

The first service provided a much-needed postal link between France and Britain from 1820, while just over a century later, the Channel saw its first car ferry service established. The first hovercraft crossing took place in 1959, preceding a flurry of such services that promised to revolutionise trans-Channel transport.

Ultimately, a more traditional approach won out, with car ferry designs growing in prominence on the trans-Channel run. Today the largest in use is the Spirit class, which operates on the Calais–Dover route. With a gross tonnage (gt) of 47,592, the 213m (698.8ft) long ships are similar in dimension to small cruise ships, and capable of transporting 2,000 passengers, 1,059 cars or 180 trucks.

These ships are dwarfed by the North Sea ferries, with the largest, linking Hull and Rotterdam, being over 59,000 gt. Look further afield, and even the North Sea fleet is dwarfed by the world's largest ferries.

Today the biggest ferry, *Color Magic*, used between Norway and Germany, exceeds 75,000 gt, comparable in size to the 1998-built *Norwegian Spirit* cruise ship.

11

RISE OF THE CRUISE SHIPS

With the initial failure of *Canberra* in the American cruise market, P&O considered whether the *Orsova* should instead remain in a cruising role. Despite the ship being of an older design, *Orsova* was smaller than *Canberra*, requiring fewer tourist-class berths to be filled in order to break even.

However, P&O had not put all of its eggs in one basket. The line had recently acquired a smaller cruise ship during its construction process. Originally designed for the fledgling Norwegian Caribbean Line, the newly acquired 17,370-grt ship was named *Spirit of London* and entered service in 1972.

The surge in interest saw P&O rethink their plans, placing *Canberra* into the British cruise market. The ship found far greater success in the UK. Meanwhile, fleet-mate *Oriana* was sent to Australia for full-time cruising in the 1980s.

While both ships are remembered fondly for their cruising service, P&O continued to struggle to run both liners at a profit. The most consistent hurdle was the large tourist-class areas, which were near impossible to fill in a cruising capacity.

The oil-hungry boilers of the P&O duo were costly to operate, particularly with fuel prices at such high levels. Both ships often cruised with whole sections of tourist class closed off to reduce costs.

Crew levels were reduced, with fewer areas of the ship needing cabin servicing, yet without the revenue from those berths the overall income of the ships was impacted. It was clear that large liners could cruise but making them profitable in their original configuration was more of a challenge.

P&O and other legacy lines were competing directly for cruise passengers with new start-ups, focused entirely on cruising. These new lines did not have the burden of past losses and old ways of thinking faced by existing lines, meaning the new generation of cruise executives were able to reimagine the passenger ship as a platform for pleasure.

An early start-up was Princess Cruises. Under the direction of Stanley McDonald, Princess Cruises chartered the 1949-built *Princess Patricia* from Canadian Pacific in 1965. One of two ships developed for Canadian Pacific's Alaskan cruising, *Princess Patricia* was named after Princess Patricia of Connaught. She was designed as a coastal steamer, with twin funnels and a single mast.

Under her Princess Cruises charter, the ship was used for pleasure voyages between Los Angeles and the Mexican Riviera. With the Canadian Pacific ship built for the cold climates of Alaska, her performance in the heat of Mexico was less than ideal, leading McDonald to look elsewhere for replacement tonnage, ultimately replacing her with *Italia* and then Costa's *Carla C*, which was marketed as *Princess Carla*.

Costa was in a position to lease old ships to Princess Cruises as they had new tonnage. This included *Eugineo C.*, which was completed in 1966. Built at the Cantieri Riuniti Dell'Adriatico yard, *Eugineo C.* featured a swan-neck bow and a Costanzi stern. Like *Rotterdam*, the ship sported twin thin funnel uptakes towards her stern and was able to adapt to a cruising role due to a cruise-friendly design.

Another notable 1960s start-up was Ensign Cruises, under the direction of Knut Kloster and Ted Arison. Kloster's 135m (443ft) long *Sunward* was utilised for a season of cruising in 1966, though the ship was built for an intended car ferry service between the UK and Gibraltar.

Sunward's cruises offered Kloster and Arison a glimpse into the cruise market, and ultimately led to both men becoming key figures in the industry. Together, the pair would pioneer Miami-based cruising.

Operating cruise ships out of Miami was initially met with much scepticism by the established operators. With many legacy shipping lines having facilities and infrastructure established at large cities such as New York, Boston and Halifax, the idea of running holiday voyages out of the relatively untried Miami market seemed foolhardy.

However here is where the differences between established lines, and new lines, was most evident. Without the sunk costs of the legacy shipping lines, new operators were free to organise their cruise itineraries any way they liked, the risk was theirs to take.

Free of this legacy burden, Arison and Kloster were able to see something that the legacy lines did not. Miami was closer to the islands of the Caribbean than New York.

Thus, passengers could take shorter pleasure voyages, and get access to the idyllic tropical islands. Shorter voyages, with less time spent steaming to and from their hubs, meant the overall cruise price was lower.

As cruise lines established more services from Florida, there was another revelation. The jet airliner was a friend, not a foe. This paradigm shift changed the way cruise holidays worked.

With airfares becoming increasingly affordable, passengers from all across the United States were able to fly to the newly established Floridian hub to board the ship – the era of fly-cruise travel was born.

Arison and Kloster ultimately parted ways, but the success of *Sunward* had planted a seed in both men's minds. Kloster would go on to head up the newly renamed Norwegian Caribbean Line, while Arison focused on developing his own cruise business.

In 1968 another brand was introduced into the cruise market, Royal Caribbean Cruise Line. The brand originated from the coming together of three Norwegian shipping companies, Anders Wilhemsen and Company, Gotaas-Larsen and I.M. Skaugen.

Under the direction of tourism executive Ed Stephan, and with funding provided by the three founding organisations, the brand commenced constructing purpose-built cruise ships, starting with the *Song of Norway*.

Built at the Wärtsilä shipyard in Helsinki, Finland, the ship's design was customised for the emerging Caribbean cruise market. Features included a shallow draft to allow easy access to small ports in the Caribbean, and an efficient diesel propulsion system that allowed a maximum speed of just under 21 knots.

Passengers had superb views of cruising ports through the large windows. The decks were wide, with a central open-air entertainment area and a terraced stern. Most strikingly, the new ship sported a raised observation lounge surrounding the aft of the funnel. Named the Viking Crown Lounge, this space became a key differentiator that allowed Royal Caribbean to stand out.

Song of Norway entered service in 1970, with her maiden voyage departing from Miami. She was quickly followed by two sister ships, *Nordic Prince* in 1971 and *Sun Viking* in 1972. All three ships were based off the same basic floorplan, giving Royal Caribbean's new fleet a sense of uniformity and commonality from the get-go.

Throughout the same time period, Norwegian Caribbean Line was also working on the development of four purpose-built cruise ships. Named *Starward*, *Skyward*, *Southward* and *Seaward*, these were all similar in design, with the third ship entering service in 1971 and *Seaward* ultimately becoming *Spirit of London* for P&O.

The following year Ted Arison launched Carnival Cruise Line. In contrast to Norwegian Caribbean Line's new tonnage, Carnival turned to the excess of retiring ocean liners to seed their cruise line ambitions.

Carnival's first ship was the 198.1m (650ft) long *Mardi Gras*, which had entered service a decade earlier as Canadian Pacific's *Empress of Canada*. The former ocean liner had been laid up in Tilbury in 1971 and was purchased by Carnival in 1972.

Mardi Gras was distinctly different from the first Norwegian and Royal Caribbean ships. Though of an ocean liner origin, the vessel had a pleasing mix of open deck spaces, public rooms, and amenities.

Additionally, a relatively short period of inactivity between her Canadian Pacific and Carnival service meant the ship's reactivation process was relatively smooth, with maintenance and servicing of the vessel remaining in good order.

Mardi Gras repositioned to the Port of Miami and was advertised by Carnival as the 'flagship of the golden fleet'. Her maiden sailing for Carnival took place on 11 March 1972, but during the departure the ship grounded. It took twenty-four hours for the ship to be freed. Subsequent inspections showed no permanent damage, allowing her to continue her maiden cruise.

Despite the challenges of *Mardi Gras*' maiden voyage, Carnival's approach quickly started to gain traction. The company boldly publicised the amenities of their ship, with less focus on the cruise itinerary in place of emphasising the fun and engaging on-board ambiance, created by an enthusiastic and dedicated cruise staff.

The cruise director was an important part of a cruise holiday, heading up a team of entertainment staff. This structure allowed for the reimagining of sea days.

Canberra (1961–97). *Canberra* was designed for the long-duration line voyages between the United Kingdom and Australia, however she enjoyed a long second-life as a cruise ship. (Andrew Sassoli-Walker/www.solentphotographer.com)

Opposite page: Clockwise from top left: *Canberra* (1961–97). A ship's bell is an important part of the heritage of the vessel, with many ships retaining their original bell throughout their career. *Canberra* sailed her whole career under her original name, with her original owners. (Andrew Sassoli-Walker/www.solentphotographer.com); *Starward* (1968–2018). *Starward* was one of a fleet of new vessels that revolutionised cruise travel. Designed and built in the 1960s for Norwegian Caribbean Line, the ship was instrumental in establishing the NCL presence in the global cruise market. (Peter Knego/www.midshipcentury.com); *Mardi Gras* (1961–2003). The 'flagship of the golden fleet' was how the fledgling Carnival Cruise Line marketed *Mardi Gras*. With ocean liner origins, the ship was highly successful in her Carnival role. (Bill Miller Collection)

Above: Clockwise from top left: *Carnivale* (1956–2008). Built for Canadian Pacific as *Empress of Britain*, the ship also sailed for the Greek Line before being acquired by Carnival. Renamed *Carnivale*, she was given a cruising refurbishment and remained with the line until 1993. (Peter Knego/www.midshipcentury.com); *Queen Elizabeth 2* (1969–2008). *QE2*'s giant bow dwarfs even the tallest onlooker. Designed in the late 1960s as a floating resort, *QE2* remained in service for thirty-nine years. (Frame & Cross); *Carnivale* (1956–2008) and *Mardi Gras* (1961–2003). The first of the Carnival Cruise Line ships. *Carnivale* (right) sails past *Mardi Gras* (left). These ships were the line's original 'Fun Ships'. (Peter Knego/www.midshipcentury.com)

Achille Lauro (1947–1994). Originally named *Willem Ruys*, the ship was rebuilt in 1965 as *Achille Lauro*, and had a troubled life. She was damaged by fire during her conversion and was later the scene of a dramatic hijacking during which a passenger was murdered. In 1994 the ship caught fire and sank off the coast of Somalia. (Peter Knego/www.midshipcentury.com)

Achille Lauro (1947–94). A much-reworked superstructure sits atop the original hull of *Willem Ruys*. *Achille Lauro*'s two funnels were greatly modified from their original design and given the white star of Flotta Lauro Lines. (Peter Knego/www.midshipcentury.com)

Apollon (1961–2003). Launched in 1960 as Canadian Pacific's *Empress of Canada*, this ship is best remembered as Carnival's *Mardi Gras*. After her Carnival sale in 1993 she cruised as *Olympic, Star of Texas, Lucky Star* and finally *Apollon*. (Peter Knego/www.midshipcentury.com)

Ted Arison tasked Farcus with creating a space aboard *Festivale* that would wow travellers, with the aim of attracting younger people to choose a cruise holiday not just for the destination, but for the ship.

The emergence of year-round cruising from Florida to the tropics created significant change for the region. As Carnival, Norwegian and Royal Caribbean increased the frequency of their voyages, Caribbean islands witnessed a boom in international visitors.

The increase in travellers visiting countries throughout the Caribbean led to the emergence of an entirely new tourist-based economy, forever changing the demographics and socioeconomics of these island nations.

As new entrants were revolutionising the cruise market, long-established lines continued to struggle. Throughout the 1960s, Cunard found it increasingly challenging to maintain viability on the transatlantic. Initially, the organisation had underestimated the threat of the jet airliner, with one Cunard director famously proclaiming, 'Flying is a fad.'

However, as the decade marched on, Cunard rethought its strategy. Under the direction of a newly appointed chair, Sir Basil Smallpeice, the line started to aggressively investigate alternative options for its flailing passenger and freight business.

Smallpeice brought a background in aviation to the table. His way of thinking challenged the status quo at Cunard, leading to the organisation forming separate joint ventures with both BOAC and Eagle Airways for flight holidays to the tropics.

Branded as BOAC-Cunard and Cunard Eagle Airways respectively, these ventures would not yield the kind of profits Cunard required to maintain its liner network but did give the business valuable insight into the fast-evolving transportation market.

At the same time, the business was developing plans for a new liner. This ship, code-named Q3, was intended to be a transatlantic liner, with some cruising considerations in the overall design.

Whereas on the ocean liners shipboard entertainment was something of a joint venture, where passengers had to rely on their own ingenuity to keep themselves entertained, aboard a Carnival cruise entertainment was the key selling point. Over time, Carnival adapted their marketing position, referring to their fleet as 'the fun ships', to emphasise their on-board approach.

P&O's failed attempt to enter the American cruise market with *Canberra* had not stopped them from exploring this area further. The line had learnt a lot from the British success of their new ship, *Spirit of London*, but rather than try and penetrate the US market with a British product, turned their sights to existing US-based cruise lines. This decision ultimately led to the 1974 acquisition of Princess Cruises. With P&O's finances behind it, the fledgling Princess operation was able to begin making plans for expansion.

Carnival expanded its footprint in 1975 with the introduction of another former Canadian Pacific liner. Originally named *Empress of Britain*, the ship was acquired from Greek interests and renamed *Carnivale*. The ship underwent a three-week cruising refurbishment, which included work by architect Joseph Farcus, with a theatre redesign among the most striking changes.

Three years later, the former S.A. *Vaal* was acquired by the line. Renamed *Festivale*, the ship was the largest yet for Carnival Cruise Line. She was treated to an extensive $30 million refurbishment, overseen by Farcus.

Ultimately Cunard would shelve the Q3 project, however learnings from the design were incorporated into a new design: Q4. The dual-purpose Q4 was shorter than the ships she replaced, with a narrower beam, allowing her to transit the Panama Canal. Her superstructure was built of aluminium, a technique used on past liners such as *Canberra*. The lighter aluminium material allowed the ship's designers to add an extra deck of passenger amenities, which boosted her cruising appeal.

The new Cunard ship would sport terraced aft decks, four swimming pools, outdoor eateries, multiple show lounges, a theatre and air conditioning throughout. Every cabin had en suite bathrooms, while the ship's large floor-to-ceiling windows offered magnificent views from the public spaces.

Built as a two-class liner, the ship could easily sail in a single class during her cruising season, allowing all passengers to enjoy all of the amenities and activities aboard the ship. This, perhaps more than anything else, would offer her the greatest chance of success.

The new Cunard ship's keel was laid down at John Brown Shipyard in 1965, the same year *Oceanic* entered service for Home Lines. Interestingly, by the time *Oceanic* joined the fleet, Home Lines had ceased operating line voyages, with *Oceanic* entering the cruise market full time. This proved the wisdom of employing a design philosophy that was versatile enough to operate cruise voyages.

The new Cunard ship was launched in 1967. Named *Queen Elizabeth 2*, the ship quickly became known as *QE2*. She entered service in 1969 and by 1970 was making enough money to allow Cunard to start repaying the loans they had taken out to build the ship. The success of *QE2*'s cruises buoyed Cunard, encouraging the line to invest in further cruise ships.

In the early 1970s Cunard acquired two new-builds: *Cunard Adventurer* and *Cunard Ambassador*. Of a similar scale to Norwegian Caribbean's ships, the vessels were used to establish Cunard in the Caribbean and Mediterranean markets. They were ultimately replaced by the larger *Cunard Countess* and *Cunard Princess*.

ACHILLE LAURO

In October 1985 the Italian-flagged *Achille Lauro* was hijacked while on a Mediterranean cruise from Genova to Egypt and Israel. Four members of the Palestine Liberation Front sailed with the ship, and with weapons they had smuggled aboard were able to seize it.

The incident commenced on 7 October, after the ship had sailed from Alexandria. The passenger complement was lower than usual, owing to a number of travellers being on an extended shore tour that was to rendezvous with the ship at a later port.

The ordeal lasted until 10 October, with the hijackers demanding that the Israeli government release several dozen Palestinian prisoners. As the situation deteriorated aboard the ship, an American passenger was executed. Having initially fled the ship, the hijackers were later apprehended aboard an Egypt Air Boeing 737, which was first trailed and then forced to land by US Navy F-14 Tomcats.

Following the incident, port security was greatly increased. Screening procedures were enhanced aboard passenger ships in order to stop weaponry being brought aboard, while unrestricted shoreside visits were curtailed.

12

POPULAR CULTURE

In 1975 Princess Cruises acquired two ships from Flagship Cruises. *Sea Venture* and *Island Venture* were 19,900-grt each and had a variety of cruise-centric design features. Most noticeable were the ships' large pool and lido decks, covered by a sliding glass roof known as a magrodome.

After being acquired by Princess Cruises, the two ships were renamed and refurbished. *Sea Venture* emerged as *Pacific Princess*, while *Island Venture* was renamed *Island Princess*.

In 1977, Princess Cruises skyrocketed to fame when the *Pacific Princess* was used as the location for the television show *The Love Boat*. Filming took place aboard both *Pacific Princess* and *Island Princess*, as well as on a series of sets, however the *Pacific Princess* exterior and name were used throughout the series.

The inclusion of a cruise ship as the location for a major television series expanded the appeal of cruising to the masses. With the show's success came increasing interest in cruising around the world, particularly when the series started airing in international markets.

In 1979 the former ocean liner *France* was acquired by Norwegian Caribbean Cruise Line for $18 million. Relocated to Bremerhaven, Germany, Kloster announced plans to convert the former transatlantic liner into the world's largest cruise ship, at a cost of close to $100 million.

Plans to utilise the giant liner as a cruise ship were widely criticised by the world's press, with many predicting it would be an unprofitable and unsuccessful white elephant. Yet, Kloster pushed on, with the ship's refurbishment continuing apace at the German yard.

Works included the redesign of public spaces, opening her up for a one-class cruising service. On-deck amenities were altered to include more space for outdoor activities and dining, while the ship's traditional livery was repainted, with a striking blue hull complemented by white and blue colours on her twin stacks.

Renamed *Norway* and registered in Oslo, the ship entered Norwegian service in 1980 to great fanfare. At a time when legacy cruise lines were still largely employing crews from their nation of origin, much attention was given to the *Norway*'s international crew, with the ship flying the United Nations flag from her bow during her inaugural season.

Island Princess (1972–2014). While enjoying less screen time than her sister ship, *Island Princess* was used extensively during the filming of The *Love Boat* television series. She commenced service as *Island Venture* and after her Princess career, sailed until 2014 under various operators. (Peter Knego/www.midshipcentury.com)

Opposite: *Pacific Princess* (1971–2013). The Love Boat, *Pacific Princess*, is beloved for taking centre stage in the popular television series. She started her career as *Sea Venture* for Flagship Cruises, and after her Princess career sailed with various owners until 2013. (Henderson & Cremer Collection)

In 1981 Royal Caribbean commenced construction of an innovative purpose-built cruise ship. Named *Song of America*, the $140 million vessel was noticeably larger than the existing Royal Caribbean fleet, with a gross tonnage of 37,500. It featured expanded passenger facilities, as well as an innovative 360-degree Viking Crown Lounge that encircled the funnel.

Carnival introduced its first new-build cruise ship, *Tropicale*, in January 1982. Built by Aalborg Værft Ålborg in Denmark at a cost of over $100 million, the ship featured a unique profile with a squared stern, angled forward superstructure and wide, open, top deck. Most striking was the addition of a stylised winged funnel, resplendent in the Carnival red, white and blue livery.

Nicknamed the 'Whale Tail', this design feature further emphasised the Carnival brand, and started a revolution in shipboard branding that would see rival lines adapt their funnel shapes and colours to become easier to recognise from a distance. Better yet, it outperformed traditional funnel designs in wind tunnel tests, meaning the branded design was better at dispersing smoke and soot away from the ship's aft decks.

The launch of *Tropicale* buoyed Carnival to commence an ambitious marketing programme with television advertising launching from 1984. These ads featured a then-newly minted Carnival ambassador, US celebrity Kathie Lee Gifford, singing lyrics espousing the benefits of the Carnival Fun Ships.

The following year, Carnival introduced the first in a trio of 46,000+ gt cruise ships. The first, *Holiday*, resembled the *Tropicale*, however the larger size allowed the ship to introduce an expanded Carnival product. She was followed by *Jubilee* in 1986 and *Celebration* in 1987.

The same year that *Celebration* entered Carnival service, Royal Caribbean launched the largest cruise ship yet built, *Sovereign of the Seas*. Built at the Chantiers de l'Atlantique shipyard in Saint-Nazaire, France, the ship's 73,700 gt eclipsed both *QE2* and *Norway* in tonnage, and although she was noticeably shorter than the elder ships, *Sovereign of the Seas* was taller.

The ship's top decks were wide, with lifeboats stored lower in the hull allowing for the top decks to overhang the boat deck. This enabled expansive entertainment areas, while the Viking Crown Lounge design was enlarged.

The new Royal Caribbean flagship entered service in 1988. Based out of Miami, the ship proved instantly popular, prompting Royal Caribbean to order two more ships of the same class.

In 1987 Carnival listed on the stock exchange, with 20 per cent of its common stock generating some $400 million for the company. This was followed by the 1989 acquisition of Holland America Line. With Carnival's acquisition, Holland America's corporate headquarters relocated to the United States and inaugurated a consolidation of cruise brands over the next two decades.

Nippon Yusen Kaisha took delivery of the Mitsubishi Heavy Industries-built cruise ship *Asuka* in 1991. At 28,856 gt she was the largest cruise ship built for the Japanese domestic market. NYK also owned the Crystal Cruises brand, which they had established in 1988. It operated the larger *Crystal Harmony*, which undertook international itineraries.

Star Cruises began operations in 1993 based out of Hong Kong. Its first two ships were converted car ferries. *Star Aquarius* and *Star Pisces* specifically catered to the Asia Pacific cruise market. In 1995 they introduced the *SuperStar Gemini*. The former *Crown Jewel* proved very popular in her new role.

Also in 1995, P&O introduced a new *Oriana*, the largest cruise ship purpose-built for the UK market. Constructed at the Meyer Werft shipyard in Papenburg, Germany, the ship was designed for longer-duration cruising from Southampton. Design features included the largest unobstructed West End-style theatre of its day, as well as a direct-drive diesel powerplant that aimed to offer speedy crossings of the often rough Bay of Biscay.

With the successful introduction of *Oriana*, P&O's UK-based cruise division finally bid the *Canberra* farewell in 1997.

Song of America (1982–). A radical new-build for Royal Caribbean Cruise Line, this ship introduced a 360-degree observation lounge on her funnel. She sailed with her original owner until 1999 when she was sold and has since cruised with various other lines. (Peter Knego/www.midshipcentury.com)

Oriana (1995–). *Oriana* was P&O's first attempt at building a contemporary cruise ship for the modern UK market. The design featured an entire deck of balcony cabins, as well as a large open-air swimming pool deck and a terraced stern. (Frame & Cross)

Canberra (1961–97). *Canberra* ended her career in 1997 when she was sold for scrap in India. The ship had gained fame for her service during the Falklands War and remained beloved by P&O regulars until her final voyage. (Peter Knego/www.midshipcentury.com)

Fairstar (1957–97). Unimposing and in many ways unremarkable, the *Fairstar* is proof that a ship is more than the sum of its parts. Originally designed as a troop carrier, she was converted for cruising by Sitmar, and became Australia's favourite cruise ship. (Henderson & Cremer Collection)

Carnival Fascination (1994–2022). The Fantasy class of cruise ships signalled a step change for Carnival, with eight built. *Carnival Fascination* was built in 1994 and cruised until her career was cut short by the COVID-19 pandemic. (Andrew Sassoli-Walker/www. solentphotographer.com)

Fair Princess (1956–2005). Designed as Cunard's transatlantic *Carinthia*, the ship was sold to Sitmar in the late 1960s and converted into a cruise ship. She later served with Princess Cruises as *Fair Princess* and retained her Princess name while cruising for P&O in Australia. (Henderson & Cremer Collection)

That year also saw the retirement of Australia's much-loved but ageing *Fairstar*. The ship was a converted Bibby Line troop transport, formerly known as *Oxfordshire*. She had been acquired by Sitmar to run the Australian immigration service and later operated cruises based out of Sydney.

When P&O acquired Sitmar Cruises in 1988, the ship was retained in the Australian market due to her popularity and marketed under the P&O Holidays brand. *Fairstar* was replaced with the *Fair Princess*. Transferred to P&O from subsidiary Princess Cruises, *Fair Princess* was in fact several years older than *Fairstar*, yet her Sitmar-era rebuilding and subsequent Princess-era refurbishments gave her superior passenger amenities.

The 1990s saw Carnival expand its cruise offering further, with the launch of the Fantasy-class ships. The 70,367 gt design was slightly smaller than the Sovereign class, and sported a somewhat more traditional profile with fewer balcony cabins and the lifeboats set high atop the superstructure.

However, the size of these ships enabled Carnival to expand its 'entertainment architecture' approach. The first vessel of this specification to enter service was *Carnival Fantasy*. Built at Finland's Kværner Masa-Yards, the ship entered the Miami market in 1990. She was followed by seven ships of the same class over the coming eight years, with each sporting a unique interior décor.

The success of the Fantasy class prompted Carnival to think bigger, and throughout the 1990s the company set about plans to push the design envelope further. In 1996 these plans culminated with the launch of the largest passenger ship yet built, *Carnival Destiny*.

At over 100,000 gt, *Carnival Destiny* was the first passenger ship to eclipse the size of Cunard's ocean liner *Queen Elizabeth*. *Carnival Destiny* introduced a radical new exterior appearance to the Carnival stable. A short and stubby bow and squared stern bookended a balcony-heavy design, greatly increasing the access to veranda accommodation compared to the Fantasy class.

Internally, the ship's deck plans offered an enlarged on-board experience. Hints of the Fantasy class could be seen in the central atrium, show lounge positioning and large 'Whale Tail' funnel, but the larger floorplan allowed for more amenities to be introduced.

Carnival Destiny (1996–). *Carnival Destiny* took the title of world's largest passenger ship in 1996 and was the first passenger ship over 100,000 gt. Today she sails as *Carnival Sunshine*. (Peter Knego/www.midshipcentury.com)

Crystal Harmony (1990–). Built by Mitsubishi Heavy Industries in Japan, the *Crystal Harmony* was the first new-build for Crystal Cruises. She was transferred to the Nippon Yusen Kaisha fleet in 2006 and sails as *Asuka II*. (Peter Knego/www.midshipcentury.com)

Costa Victoria (1996–2021). Built at Bremer Vulkan, *Costa Victoria* entered service in 1996. She was supposed to have a sister ship, *Costa Olympia*, but the second vessel was completed as *Norwegian Sky* for NCL. *Costa Victoria* was scrapped during the COVID-19 pandemic. (Vicki Cross)

Norway (1962–2003). A sad end to a great ship, the *Norway* is seen here at rest on the beaches of Alang, India, where she was scrapped. The ship experienced a fatal boiler explosion in 2003 and was sold to the breakers in 2006. (Peter Knego/www. midshipcentury.com)

MSC Opera (2004–). The 59,058 gt *MSC Opera* was the flagship of MSC Cruises from 2004–06. She was among the first new builds for MSC, but today is dwarfed by their current flagship, the 215,863 gt *World Europa*. (Vicki Cross)

The 1998 cruise year was tough for Cunard. The company had grown to become a relatively large cruise line, with a total of eleven passenger ships and numerous river cruising vessels under its banner by 1994. But the continuing rise of large cruise lines along with well-funded, smaller-scale premium brands combined to squeeze Cunard's market share.

By the mid-1990s strong and clear branding had become critical for the success of cruise lines and the Cunard brand had lost its way. Carnival Cruise Line, Norwegian Cruise Line and Royal Caribbean had mastered branding. Strong brand management was also evident at Holland America, Costa and Princess Cruises. P&O's cruising divisions had clearly defined brand positions in both the UK and Australia.

With a strong brand, customers knew what to expect when engaging with the cruise line. It made it easier for lines to connect with their market segment, as their customers understood the core brand elements that would be evident aboard each of the line's ships.

In its growth Cunard had become an undefined brand. Cunard had been under the control of Trafalgar House Co. since the 1970s, however in 1996 it was acquired by Kværner as part of a deal to buy Trafalgar House. Things worsened for Cunard over the following two years, so much so that by the time QE2 set sail on her 1998 world cruise the line was for sale.

In 1997, James Cameron's blockbuster movie *Titanic* catapulted transatlantic travel into the heart of popular culture. Millions of moviegoers sat mesmerised at the elegance and size of the *Titanic*, witnessing the romance of a transatlantic crossing.

At the height of the movie's success, QE2 was the only passenger ship undertaking regularly scheduled transatlantic crossings. Better yet, her owner was for sale. The stars aligned for Cunard, and Carnival Corporation bid $800 million for a majority stake in the company.

The acquisition was completed in April 1998, with Cunard joining the Carnival stable. Carnival merged Cunard operations with Seabourn Cruise Line in 1999 to offer improved economies of scale and set about realigning the positioning and fleet of each brand.

Cunard's fleet was reduced to two British-style ocean liners, QE2 and *Caronia*, the latter previously sailing as *Vistafjord*. They were marketed under the new slogan: 'The most famous ocean liners in the world', with the brand fully embracing its rich history at every touchpoint.

Seabourn acquired three of the former Cunard luxury cruise ships and refurbished them to supplement their existing fleet of luxury super yachts. All six Seabourn vessels were marketed under a unified platform of unmatched luxury and personalised service.

The tactic worked, and in the coming years both brands successfully carved out unique market positions for themselves in the cluttered cruise industry.

As the twentieth century drew to a close, a new race for size was under way. *Carnival Destiny* had proven that cruise ships of 100,000 gt were not only possible, but profitable, opening the doors to an array of contenders for the title of 'world's largest cruise ship'.

Princess Cruises was the first brand to challenge *Carnival Destiny*'s title. The 1998 *Grand Princess* ushered in an entirely new style of vessel for the brand.

Built at Fincantieri Cantieri Navali Italiani Monfalcone, Italy, *Grand Princess*'s external profile caught the attention of even the most casual observer. Stepped, semicircular forward decking was topped by an oversized bridge structure, complete with large support struts that gave the ship a commanding forward profile.

The ship sported a large top deck, from which a glass-enclosed walkway angled up to an oversized observation lounge. The walkway contained a moving travelator, as well as space for passengers to walk if they preferred. The observation space at the aft of the ship sat atop an almost vertical stern. It offered remarkable views over the wake, but its appearance resembled a handle, and earned the Grand-class design a less than flattering nickname: 'the shopping trolley'.

Star Cruises greatly expanded its offering from 1998 with the introduction of their first new build, the 75,338 gt *SuperStar Leo*. Built at Meyer Werft in Papenburg, she was joined the following year by a sister ship, *SuperStar Virgo*.

REFURBISHMENTS

Cruise ships generally have an expected service life of between twenty-five and forty years. Just like a car, a ship requires regular maintenance to keep everything in top working condition. But sometimes these overhauls go even further.

Following the First World War, many of the world's largest ocean liners were converted to burn oil, rather than coal. This involved a huge amount of work, including replacing the existing rivets with countersunk rivets and dividing the existing coal bunkers with bulkheads to allow oil to be stored instead. The process took months and was a big investment for the shipping lines.

Another major re-engining project was the conversion of *QE2* from turbine power to diesel electric in 1986–87. This involved the replacement of the ship's original steam turbine plant as well as associated machinery including the propellers and propeller shafts.

In addition to mechanical and engineering overhauls, ships are given interior refreshes on a fairly regular basis. This can include anything from replacing the carpets and soft furnishings to entirely reimagining the design of a space. *Norwegian Spirit* was given a $100 million refurbishment in 2020, modernising and improving the interior spaces and accommodation.

Refurbishments keep ships profitable by ensuring that passengers are not disappointed by a lack of modern amenities. Refurbishments can also make ships more profitable, by introducing new spaces and increasing the passenger complement.

Stretching the ship or adding a new section to the middle increases the number of passengers that can be carried, as well as allowing for new public spaces. Examples of ships that have been stretched are Royal Caribbean's *Enchantment of the Seas*, MSC's *Sinfonia* and Fred Olsen's former cruise ship *Braemar*.

Another way to increase the passenger capacity of a ship is to add prefabricated blocks of cabins to non-revenue-generating areas of the ship. This has been seen across numerous Vista class ships in the Carnival Corporation, as well as being a key feature of the 1990 refit of *Norway*.

13

THE CRUISING BOOM

With the popularity of cruising booming, passenger lines continued to seek out new ways to differentiate and diversify their product offering.

One way to do this was through acquisitions, with Royal Caribbean acquiring Celebrity Cruise Line in 1997. Celebrity had been developed in 1988 as a cruising division of Chandris. New builds *Horizon* and *Zenith* had proven popular, while the larger Century class was under development at the time of the acquisition, with the class leader *Century* having already been delivered.

The following year, the definition of what constituted a cruise was further expanded with the inaugural voyage of *Disney Magic*. The 83,969 gt ship was the first of two for the Disney Cruise Line and introduced a truly immersive experience at sea.

With an on-board philosophy reminiscent of Disney's land-based resorts, the ship was designed with extensive input from Disney's Imagineers, and the result was striking. Twin funnels sat atop a white superstructure. A dark hull featured exposed yellow anchors and customised artwork on both the bow and stern, giving these cruise ships the appearance of a traditional ocean liner.

Internally, the ships featured art deco blended with Disney styling. Theming from Disney's various film franchises are found throughout.

Disney also acquired a ninety-nine-year lease on a small cay in the Bahamas. Renamed Castaway Cay, the island was developed with themed retail stores and restaurants, and acts as an extension of the on-board experience.

The emergence of private islands had started with Norwegian Cruise Line's Great Stirrup Cay in 1977. The island was used as a way to differentiate Norwegian's cruises from those of its competitors.

In the years since, a variety of cruise lines have acquired long-term leases for Bahamian and Caribbean islands, with Carnival, Holland America, Royal Caribbean, Regent Seven Seas, Princess Cruise Line, Azamara, Oceania, MSC and Virgin Voyages among the brands that utilise them.

For decades, private islands required a tender ride from the cruise ship, and Disney was the first line to offer docking facilities from 1998. This was achieved through an extensive and expensive dredging process but enables a smoother transfer of passengers ashore at Castaway Cay. Subsequent upgrades have seen docking facilities added to many other private islands.

In 1998 Cunard announced it would build its first ship in a generation. The news was surprising, as the new ship was planned to be built as an ocean liner, and to undertake regular transatlantic crossings.

Under the direction of Carnival's chief naval architect, Stephen Payne, designs for the new Cunarder (nicknamed Project Queen Mary) were formulated. As this ship was to take over the regular transatlantic schedule from *QE2*, Payne was determined to ensure the vessel was built to a true ocean liner standard.

However, ship design had moved on considerably since the last ocean liners were built decades ago. There had been a revolution in shipbuilding techniques, with prefabrication significantly improving the efficiency and speed at which a passenger ship could be built.

Additionally, travellers had grown accustomed to balcony-grade accommodation. This meant Project Queen Mary would need to offer a high proportion of balcony cabins in order to be competitive in her dual-purpose cruising role.

The ship's dimensions grew to accommodate the various needs of a one-off, dual-purpose, modern transatlantic liner. By the time the first steel was cut at the Chantiers d'Atlantique shipyard in France, the vessel had grown on paper to become the longest, widest and tallest passenger ship yet ordered, with a gross tonnage of 151,400.

Cunard's new ocean liner was named *Queen Mary 2* before the first steel was cut. The final design incorporated four Rolls-Royce pods, with two fixed and two able to rotate.

Disney Magic (1998–). *Disney Magic* was the first ship in the Disney Cruises fleet and represented a significant leap in design, with an external profile created to echo the appearance of a classic ocean liner. (Andrew Sassoli-Walker/www.solentphotographer.com)

Queen Mary 2 (2004–). The first true transatlantic liner built in a generation, *Queen Mary 2* was the largest, longest, tallest, and widest passenger ship when she was delivered to Cunard. (Frame & Cross)

Voyager of the Seas (1998–). Royal Caribbean's first 100,000+ gt ship, *Voyager of the Seas*, established a trend of building larger cruise ships that Royal Caribbean still follow to this day. (Frame & Cross)

Early podded propulsion was driven using hydraulics. These pods had an issue with 'hunting', where the pods would wobble. Designers were concerned that this wobble would cause issues when operating at high speeds, essentially causing *Queen Mary 2* to 'snake' across the Atlantic. Rolls-Royce subsequently developed an electric steering system, eliminating the 'hunting' issue.

In 1999, Royal Caribbean introduced its 137,276 gt *Voyager of the Seas*. The first in the Voyager class, the ship was built at the Kværner Masa-Yards, in Turku New Shipyard in Finland and was the largest cruise ship in the world at the time of her launch.

The new generation of 100,000+ gt cruise ships took the concept of the passenger ship to a new level. The sheer size of these vessels allowed for internal spaces to be reimagined yet again, with *Voyager of the Seas* introducing the first on-board ice-skating rink, as well as a rock-climbing wall on the aft decks.

But size wasn't the only measure of innovation, and from the 1980s there had been a boost in the number of smaller purpose-built cruise vessels and expedition ships.

Luxury cruise lines often utilise smaller ships with a lower passenger complement. This allows for a higher crew-to-passenger ratio, which affords more attentive service. The lower passenger numbers create a more exclusive experience, with many luxury brands providing inclusions in the base fare such as drinks, alternative dining venues and even shore tours. These additional perks are offset by higher fares, enabling these lines to make a profit.

Additionally, smaller ships can visit a wider variety of ports, with less need to run time-consuming tender services during the voyage.

Sea Goddess Cruises were among the early pioneers in this space, with a duo of 4,253 gt super yachts. Launched in 1984 and 1985, the venture had mixed fortunes. With just three passenger decks, they were undoubtedly small. Yet their 112 passengers were served by ninety-five crew, offering a truly personalised and intimate experience.

Seabourn Cruise Line was founded in 1986 and established itself as a stalwart in the luxury cruise market starting with a duo of 9,000 gt ships that were later joined by a third vessel of similar specifications acquired from Royal Viking Line.

Silversea Cruises is another well-known luxury brand that utilises smaller ships to great effect. Formed in 1994, its first ship was the *Silver Cloud* and it was joined the following year by *Silver Wind*.

The drive to tap into the luxury cruise market led to rapid expansion for some lines, including Renaissance Cruise Line. Established in the late 1980s, the brand had operated a fleet of 4,000 gt cruise ships until a massive new-build project was committed to in the 1990s. This venture saw the construction of eight 30,000 gt cruise ships named *R One* to *R Eight*.

Built at Chantiers de l'Atlantique, the vessels were delivered between 1998 and 2001, when the line collapsed. Despite this, the design of the ships was sound, and offered a fine balance of size, space and amenities. The R-class have been sought after in the years since, with ships from this class operating for Princess, HAPAG-Lloyd, P&O Cruises, Delphin Seereisen, Pullmantur, Oceania and Azamara.

P&O continued to expand its cruise business through the final years of the twentieth century, acquiring AIDA in 1999. In 2000, the business spun off its cruising division to form P&O-Princess, which oversaw P&O Cruises UK, P&O Cruises Australia, Princess Cruises and AIDA. The organisation added the river cruise line A'Rosa to its stable in 2001.

A majority share of Norwegian Cruise Line was acquired by Star Cruises in 2000. This led to a number of ships being transferred between the brands over the following decade, including the incomplete *SuperStar Libra* and *SuperStar Scorpio*, which entered service as the *Norwegian Star* and *Norwegian Dawn* respectively.

In 2003, Carnival Corporation expanded significantly when it merged with P&O-Princess. The merger included all of the P&O-Princess brands but was distinct from the larger P&O Steam Navigation Co., which still owned and operated ferries, ports and container ships.

By the time *Queen Mary 2* entered service in 2004, there were already plans for larger cruise ships in the works. The first such example was Royal Caribbean's 156,271 gt *Freedom of the Seas*.

The once seemingly impassable 100,000+ gt barrier was now a distant memory, and the next challenge for cruise lines was whether the 200,000+ gt barrier was possible. Royal Caribbean took on the challenge, ordering the US$1.4 billion *Oasis of the Seas* in early 2006.

The scale of the Oasis class is immense. Its gross tonnage of 226,838 is achieved thanks to a 360m (1,181ft) long hull that rises 72m (236ft) above the waterline. Sixteen passenger decks can accommodate 5,606 passengers, making the *Oasis of the Seas* more akin to a skyscraper than passenger liners of old. The ship's design employed telescoping funnels, allowing the ship's height to be reduced for passage under bridges, while a modern azipod propulsion system allows the ship to achieve an impressive 24 knots.

While the liners of old were hindered by their large size, making cruising challenging, *Oasis of the Seas* is specifically built for dense and well-established cruise markets, thus the scale of her dimensions work in her favour. Internally, the ship is divided into seven distinct 'neighbourhoods', which allows for improved passenger flow and functionality and brings the design the closest yet to that of a floating city.

Azamara Journey (2000–). Commencing her career as Renaissance Cruises' *R Six*, the ship sailed for Pullmantur Cruises before being acquired by Azamara in 2007. (Frame & Cross)

Coral Geographer (2021–). With a capacity of just ninety-nine guests, *Coral Geographer* is specifically designed for small-ship cruising. She caters to travellers who appreciate the smaller vessel's ability to cruise waterways inaccessible to large ships. (Frame & Cross)

AIDAperla (2017–). Built at the Japanese Mitsubishi Shipbuilding yard, *AIDAperla* sports a straight bow reminiscent of the liners of days gone by. AIDA is just one of many cruise lines that use distinctive hull art to differentiate their brand. (Frame & Cross)

Anthem of the Seas (2015–). The Quantum-class *Anthem of the Seas*, berthed alongside a collection of waiting tour buses. The ease for passengers to take day tours of cruise ports is one of the appeals of cruise holidays. (Frame & Cross)

Oasis of the Seas (2009–). The giant *Oasis of the Seas* was the first in the Oasis class, and the first passenger ship to exceed 200,000 gt. From the stern, her design is barely recognisable as a successor to the ocean liners. (Frame & Cross)

Amenities are plentiful, with the ship featuring a central park complete with gardens, a central boardwalk, a zipline, an ice-skating rink and even an aqua theatre. The broad range of facilities make the ship the destination.

So successful was the Oasis class that a further five ships were ordered by the line. Subsequently, Royal Caribbean has upscaled the design even further, with the 250,800 gt *Icon of the Seas* entering service in 2023.

The year 2012 marked the 100th anniversary of the loss of *Titanic*. The year was touted as an opportunity to remember the loss, while also showcasing the significant improvements in safety of life at sea achieved in the years since the disaster.

However, 2012 got off to an inauspicious start when Costa Cruises' 114,147 gt *Costa Concordia* ran aground off the coast of Giglio, Italy, with 4,229 people aboard. The ship was travelling along the Italian coast, outbound from Civitavecchia.

At around 9:45 p.m. on the evening of 13 January the ship struck rocks near Giglio, causing severe flooding, which entered the engine spaces, causing electrical failures throughout the ship. The loss of power left the ship adrift and listing, with it finally settling near Punta Gabbianara and capsizing.

The evacuation of the ship was hampered by the loss of power and the ship's list. Passengers and crew worked together in an attempt to evacuate, with some passengers ending up stranded on the ship's hull. As the situation aboard worsened, some people jumped into the ocean in an attempt to leave the ship. The captain left the ship before the evacuation was complete.

By daybreak the scale of the situation was apparent. The ship was resting half submerged on its starboard side, with the port side damage facing upwards. The size of the tear in the ship's hull was unmistakable, and tragically thirty-two people perished in the disaster.

Costa Concordia highlighted the need to further reform bridge management aboard passenger ships. Sail by salutes, whereby a ship leaves the pre-planned course to sail close to an island or port, were curtailed ahead of the official report into the incident.

Of the passengers on board, 600 had joined *Costa Concordia* in Civitavecchia. The recently embarked passengers had not been mustered for boat drill prior to the ship's departure. The SOLAS requirement then in effect was to ensure muster drills were conducted within twenty-four hours of departure.

As *Costa Concordia*'s sinking took place during the first night at sea, those passengers had not yet attended the muster briefing. Following the disaster, the Cruise Lines International Association (CLIA) instructed all member cruise lines to conduct emergency muster drills for all embarking passengers before the ship sets sail.

Bridge access was also reviewed. Looking to the aviation industry for inspiration, rules for a 'sterile' bridge environment, limiting distractions, were implemented.

In addition, bridge command set-up was modified aboard many cruise lines. The reformed protocol saw an overview officer given authority to interject if poor decision-making was witnessed by those commanding the ship, regardless of their rank.

This is similar to an aircraft's crew resource management model, limiting the 'total control' a captain or senior officer has if it is apparent that their decision-making capability is in question.

The *Costa Concordia* disaster was broadcast globally, with the subsequent inquiries and prosecution being well covered. European cruise lines experienced a brief drop in forward bookings, particularly Costa Cruises. However, by mid-2012 forward bookings were starting to recover, despite an economic downturn in Europe caused by a debt crisis.

The following year, *Carnival Triumph* was in the headlines after an engine room fire caused power failures throughout the ship. The loss of power led to high temperatures aboard, while the vacuum flush toilet system failed.

This led to sewage discharge throughout the ship, causing understandable distress for all aboard, but fortunately all passengers and crew were able to depart the ship without any lasting injuries.

Throughout the last thirty years, the consolidation of the cruise industry has led to the emergence of massive cruise conglomerates.

As of 2023, Carnival Corporation operates the most brands, with AIDA, Carnival Cruise Line, Cunard, Costa Cruises, Holland America, Princess Cruises, P&O Cruises UK, P&O Cruises Australia and Seabourn. The corporation operates over 100 cruise ships.

Royal Caribbean Group has also become a large player, operating the Royal Caribbean International, Celebrity Cruises and Silversea Cruises brands, while Norwegian Cruise Line Holdings has NCL, Oceania and Regent Seven Seas under its banner.

The meteoric rise of European cruising has seen MSC Cruises boom in recent years, and it is ranked as one of the largest cruise lines in the world by passengers carried, behind Royal Caribbean International and Carnival Cruise Line, but ahead of NCL.

Boutique ships have continued to expand their presence worldwide. An economic drive to tap into new markets has led this development, with lines looking to leverage a desire from passengers to explore unique and unusual destinations.

Coral Expeditions is one such company. Developed in the 1980s as a small ship Great Barrier Reef experience, the organisation tapped into an unmet need to offer Australian cruises to unique local landmarks best viewed from the decks of a ship.

Debuting in 1984, the line ran a converted submarine chaser named *Coral Princess*. The ship offered cruises off the east coast of Queensland, which proved successful enough to allow for the construction of a purpose-built expedition ship, *Coral Discoverer*.

Built at the NQEA Shipbuilders in Cairns, Australia, the ship measures a modest 1,838 gt. But like the giant *Icon of the Seas*, *Coral Discoverer* was built specifically to cater for its unique market segment.

Small enough to enter the pristine gorges of the Kimberley region, the ship can offer its small complement of passengers a truly remarkable experience, allowing them to get closer to Australia's natural wonders than ever before. So successful was the concept that a further two vessels were built: *Coral Adventurer* and *Coral Geographer*.

Sea Cloud (1931–). Built in Germany in the early 1930s, *Sea Cloud* is a barque with four masts and a bowsprit. After a varied career, she was acquired by Schiffahrtsgesellschaft Sea Cloud mbH & Co. in the late 1970s. (Frame & Cross)

Balmoral (1988–). *Balmoral*, pictured in Southampton, entered service in 1988 as Royal Cruise Line's *Crown Odyssey*. She later sailed as *Norwegian Crown* for NCL, *Crown Odyssey* (again) for Star Cruises' Orient Lines and finally *Balmoral* for Fred Olsen. (Frame & Cross)

Majestic Princess (2017–). The third ship in the Royal class, *Majestic Princess* is over 144,000 gt. The ship, seen in Sydney, wears the Princess Cruises livery, including a giant 'sea witch' logo on the bow. (Frame & Cross)

Opposite page:
Top: *Le Lapérouse* (2018–). The first ship of Ponant's Explorers class, *Le Lapérouse*'s hull was built in Romania and towed to Norway for completion and fit-out. She can undertake expedition cruises and world voyages. (Frame & Cross)
Bottom:*Celebrity Silhouette* (2011–). The fourth of five Solstice-class ships, *Celebrity Silhouette* is seen in 2019 in her original livery. The X logo on the ship's funnel dates to Celebrity's origins as an offshoot of Chandris. (Frame & Cross)

Norwegian Spirit (1998–). Starting her career in 1998 as Star Cruises' *SuperStar Leo*, the *Norwegian Spirit* has sailed with NCL since 2004. In 2020, the ship was given a $100 million refurbishment to extend her service life for a further twenty years. (Frame & Cross)

Other cruise brands differentiate in different ways. Windstar was founded the same year as Coral Expeditions and wowed the world by launching the *Wind Star*. A 5,307 gt cruise ship, *Wind Star* is a motorised sailing yacht, employing both engines and sails in a style reminiscent of the first steamships. The ship's modest size and unique configuration proved popular, allowing the brand to build two more ships of the same class.

Sea Dream Yachtclub is another example of a boutique small ship approach. Created in 2001, the brand acquired the *Seabourn Goddess 1* and *Seabourn Goddess 2* from Seabourn Cruise Line.

Cruise lines also developed in a range of previously untapped markets. From 1988, Compagnie du Ponant commenced operations, offering French cruises with *Le Ponant*, a three-masted barque. The luxury yacht proved popular in the market, allowing the brand to expand with more traditional luxury expedition cruise ships.

Today the business operates twelve ships, all under 20,000 gt with the exception of *Le Commandant Charcot*, which at 30,000 gt has an innovative hybrid-electric powerplant, and a polar-class hull.

THE ENVIRONMENTAL IMPACT OF PASSENGER SHIPS

Over the years the general public has become more aware of the environmental impacts of commercial shipping. This has led to increasing demands for improvement in the way ships are operated, especially as relates to passenger ships.

In 1999 Greenpeace made headlines protesting against the use of tributyltin hull paint on *QE2*. Tributyltin (TBT) was an anti-fouling additive, used from the 1970s, but it also poisoned the marine life around the ship, especially when the ship was being cleaned. Though effective at stopping the spread of marine life from one location to another, its overall impact on the environment was negative and TBT has been banned in ships' paint since 2008.

Another environmental impact is the emissions caused by fossil fuel-burning ships. Originally powered by coal, then by oil and diesel, ships produce significant emissions when under way. They also remain under their own power when alongside in ports. Many ports have introduced emission regulations, to try to limit the air pollution in areas that are often very close to residential zones. These regulations are not standardised and differ from port to port. Furthermore, there are often exemptions or different regulations depending on the age of the ship and the type of fuel used.

The Cruise Lines International Association (CLIA) partners have committed to a 2030 target for reducing cruise ship emissions by 40 per cent from 2008 levels. Currently some new-build ships are being constructed with liquefied natural gas (LNG) powerplants, as this is considered a cleaner fuel. They are also investigating the use of alternative sustainable fuels and hybrid options.

Though those ideas are still in the research phase, cold ironing is becoming more viable in a number of ports. This is the process where a ship is 'plugged in' to shoreside power while in port. This allows for the ship's engines to be turned off, reducing emissions. If the power is being generated by renewable sources this can be a great improvement in emissions overall.

Other environmental impacts that are more closely linked to passenger shipping than any other type of shipping are those that directly relate to the number of people carried aboard by these ships. This includes waste management.

Food waste is generally combusted or ground up very finely, before being mixed with sea water and discharged into the ocean in permitted areas. Packaging waste, on the other hand, is sorted for recycling ashore. Sadly, there have been many cases over the years where packaging has been dumped directly into the oceans.

Water treatment plants are another aspect of waste management. Passenger ships must deal with both sewage and grey water produced by both passengers and crew, as well as bilge water, which is more typically defined as water that accumulates at the bottom of the ship and often contains oil and other chemicals. There are regulations about the quality of wastewater that can be released into the ocean. There are also regulations about where it can be dumped. Bilge water, for example, is supposed to be thoroughly cleaned to remove oil and chemicals, before being discharged. Alternatively, this water is stored and then pumped off the ship for processing onshore.

There have been multiple environmental violations by cruise lines over the years. These range from discharging hazardous materials and dumping plastics in the ocean to damaging coral reefs and striking whales due to travelling too fast near a pod.

While promoting green credentials has become a marketing ploy for many companies, not just in the shipping industry, there is still a long way to go before it is truly sustainable. Greener solutions are often more expensive, making them less appealing to corporations focused on their bottom line, but ultimately the ocean has to be protected if cruising is to continue long term.

14

COLLAPSE AND RESURRECTION

The year 2019 was a bumper one for cruise lines. Some 29.7 million passengers took a cruise that year, which represented a 4.1 per cent increase on the previous year. It was expected that the 2020 year would be even better, with some analysts predicting 5 per cent growth.

However, 2020 would prove to be the hardest year in the cruise industry's history, due to the crippling effect of the COVID-19 pandemic. From March 2020, the cruise industry entered into a pause in cruising operations, leading to an effective shutdown of the industry.

Originally expected to last only a few months, the initial shutdown was considered 'voluntary'. Cruise ships had been experiencing COVID outbreaks aboard since February, with varying degrees of severity.

Diamond Princess's February 2020 Japanese cruise was cut short when an outbreak caused hundreds of people to fall ill. The ship was detained at Yokohama for twenty days and became the focus of intense media scrutiny.

Several other cruise ships had outbreaks of COVID aboard, including *Westerdam*, *Braemar* and *Costa Luminosa*. Cruise lines were initially challenged by the management of COVID aboard ships. Rapid Antigen Testing was still many months away, as were vaccines. Faced with outbreaks aboard, lines implemented quarantine procedures based on experience with other diseases such as Norovirus.

However, COVID proved to be more transmissible than Norovirus, particularly through air, leading to widespread outbreaks aboard. This led to CLIA cruise lines entering into a voluntary pause of operations on 14 March 2020.

Several days later, the *Ruby Princess* docked in Sydney, where passengers disembarked the ship. It was subsequently discovered that hundreds of passengers were infected with COVID. Many of the infected passengers unknowingly travelled to other destinations across Australia, leading to a series of outbreaks across the country. As such, the ship became the centre of a controversial public debate.

As the shutdown took place, cruise ships made their way to anchorage points across the world. Crews were stranded aboard the vessels for many months, while the global transportation network collapsed due to lack of demand, driven by government-mandated lockdowns.

Prior to the pandemic, ageing cruise ships had often remained in operation due to the intense demand for a cruise holiday. However, as the pause dragged on, cruise lines started to feel intense strain on their finances.

This led to many older ships being retired from service. Dramatic scenes of cruise ships being beached at the scrapyards of Aliaga, Turkey, and Alang, India, were broadcast on international news networks, while for several months, articles and videos about cruise ship scrapping attracted hundreds of thousands of views.

The pause in operations and subsequent financial strain led to the collapse of several cruise lines, including Pullmantur, CMV, Jaleesh Cruises, Star Cruises, Genting Cruises and Crystal Cruises. Some of these brands, such as Crystal, have rebounded, but most were lost forever.

Several cruise lines were planning to launch new ships in 2020 and 2021. However, with no passengers, new builds were delivered to cruise lines and sent into immediate lay-up.

Perhaps the most dramatic example of this was the 2020 launch of Virgin Voyages. With an official launch date of 1 April 2020, the newly established brand had just taken delivery of *Scarlet Lady*.

At 110,000 gt, the ship is a significant size. Virgin Voyages set about reimagining the cruise experience with the design of this ship, and purposefully challenged the status quo by hiring non-ship designers to help create a unique and unconventional on-board experience.

Built at Fincantieri Sestri Ponente, Italy, *Scarlet Lady* arrived in the UK during March 2020 for a media cruise. Having successfully completed that voyage, the ship headed for its home port of Miami, arriving as the cruise pause commenced. As such, the ship was unable to enter service until mid-2021.

The delay in maiden voyages was a familiar experience shared by a number of cruise brands. *Celebrity Apex*, P&O's *Iona*, Carnival's *Mardi Gras* and *Enchanted Princess* were among the ships impacted.

When cruising resumed throughout the second half of 2021 and early 2022, a number of changes had been implemented aboard. Masks, social distancing and a requirement to be vaccinated were among the most noticeable changes, however behind the scenes cruise lines had adapted and amended operations, learning from the pandemic.

Hospitals were upgraded with quarantine facilities, including negative pressure spaces to supress the spread of airborne viruses. Air conditioning flow was reviewed, and isolation practices were implemented for those passengers found to be sick while travelling. When cruising resumed, most cruise lines implemented strict social distancing in crowded spaces, while HEPA filters were fitted throughout the ship, especially in areas of potential crowding such as lifts.

Throughout 2022, the cruise industry slowly rebounded. Gradually, cruise ship capacity was increased, and nearly all jurisdictions had reopened borders to cruise ships by early 2023.

With cruising resuming, the new-build ships were introduced for the first time. These included some innovative designs, with several cruise ships sporting new, greener powerplants.

Most noticeable is the slow shift towards LNG-powered cruise ships, which produce up to 25 per cent less carbon and nitrogen emissions.

In the face of the worsening climate crisis, there is increasing pressure on cruise ship operators to hasten the adoption of cleaner fuel sources. To support this, the utilisation of cold ironing is becoming more widespread (see The Environmental Impact of Passenger Ships, p.179).

Miami's cruise port is leading this transformation, with a significant shore power system being developed to service ships across various terminals at the port, while other ports such as Seattle, Sydney and Southampton are developing similar systems.

Today, there are hundreds of cruise ships in service. While the most obvious of these are the biggest ships, there are many others operating in niche markets. This includes expedition ships, polar voyages, ice breakers, luxury ships, budget ships, all-inclusive cruising, adults-only cruising and themed voyages.

Combination cruise ships, such as those of the Hurtigruten Line and Aranui, combine passenger voyages with essential supply runs, while ferries continue to operate in many different places around the world.

Whether passenger ships will always be in existence is unknown, but what is certain is that they have a rich and diverse history and have made a huge impact on the way our world is today. From mass migration, to war, to a luxury holiday, passenger ships have been at the centre of many human experiences for millennia. It is likely that they will continue to do so. At least for the foreseeable future.

MSC Musica (2006–). The first of MSC's Musica-class ships, *MSC Musica*'s boxy stern is juxtaposed with the stepped design of Oceania's *Sirena* and the terraces of TUI's *Marella Dream*. (Frame & Cross)

Ruby Princess (2008–). One of Princess Cruises' Crown-class cruise ships, *Ruby Princess* shares a general arrangement and design with the Grand, Caribbean and Gem classes. (Frame & Cross)

Opposite page:
Top: *Vesterålen* (1983–). Running services on the Norwegian coast, *Vesterålen* is part of the Hurtigruten Coastal Express, which includes calls at Geirangerfjord on Norway's west coast. (Frame & Cross)
Bottom: *Oceanic* (1965–2012). Built for Home Lines, *Oceanic* was intended to run services as a two-class liner, but was easily operational as a one-class cruise ship. She sailed with Home Lines, Premier Cruises, Pullmantur and finally Peace Boat. (Frame & Cross)

Right: *Scarlet Lady* (2020–). Entering service on media familiarisation cruises just before the global cruise pause, *Scarlet Lady* was the first in a new fleet of ships built for Virgin Voyages. She resumed cruising in 2021. (Andrew Sassoli-Walker/ www.solentphotographer.com)

Disney Magic (1998–) and *Queen Mary 2* (2004–). Although both ships appear to be ocean liners, only one was built to undertake line voyages. Disney's cruise ships are all designed to resemble liners of old, while *QM2* was built to sail the transatlantic route regularly. (Andrew Sassoli-Walker/www. solentphotographer.com)

Aurora (2000–). During the cruise pause of 2020 many ships were clustered off the coast of the UK at anchorages near Southampton, Babbacombe, Torquay and Bournemouth. (Andrew Sassoli-Walker/ www.solentphotographer.com)

Radiance of the Seas (2001–). The class leader of the Radiance class, *Radiance of the Seas* is powered by gas turbines, making her carbon footprint lower than many other cruise ships. (Frame & Cross)

Coral Princess (2003–). The first of two Coral-class cruise ships built for Princess Cruises, *Coral Princess* was specifically designed small enough to transit the original locks of the Panama Canal, making her a highly flexible global cruise ship. (Frame & Cross)

Britannia (2015–). P&O Cruises' only Royal-class ship, *Britannia* shares many external traits with her Princess Cruises' counterparts. The ship's design includes many decks of balcony cabins, and upon her debut in 2015 she took the title of Flagship from P&O Cruises' *Oriana*. (Frame & Cross)

Clockwise from top left: *Aurora* (2000–). *Aurora* was the last passenger ship built for the Peninsular & Oriental Steam Navigation Co., and entered service only a few years before the P&O-Princess merger with Carnival Corporation. (Frame & Cross); *Queen Victoria* (2007–). Cunard's *Queen Victoria* features a reinforced bow to enable the ship to undertake direct transatlantic crossings with more regularity than most cruise ships. The ship is also often sent on world cruises. (Frame & Cross); *Queen Victoria* (2007–). *Queen Victoria* at sea in her original configuration, before the 2017 addition of a block of cabins on her stern that removed the aft terraced appearance. (Frame & Cross)

300 EMPTY CRUISE SHIPS

When the cruise industry entered a voluntary pause of operations in March of 2020, few realised just how long that pause was going to last. For the travelling public, not being able to go on their planned holidays was a big disappointment, but for the cruise lines there were major logistical challenges to be overcome.

In many cases passengers were asked to leave ships prior to the ending of their cruises. Cruise lines then had to figure out how to repatriate these passengers to their homes. This often involved flying passengers back to their home port. Some ships, such as QM2, which was in the middle of its world cruise when the pause was announced, sailed back to the UK with passengers still aboard who were unable to fly home. The journey was nothing like the cruise they had been enjoying up until that point, with entertainment, dining and passenger services seriously curtailed.

Once the passengers were all off there were other issues to deal with. This included finding alternative uses for the food that had been ordered for cruises that were no longer going to take place.

One of the main issues the cruise lines faced was what to do with their ships. With more than 300 cruise ships in operation at the time of the cruise pause there were not enough berths available for all of the ships to be brought into port. Instead, the ships shared anchorages around the world, often far from their usual ports of call.

The ships still needed to pull into port from time to time to restock provisions and, as the pause was extended, to exchange crew. They also needed to travel out to sea to discharge wastewater and bring on clean water for use aboard.

Crew repatriation for non-essential personnel took place from August 2020, when it became clear that things wouldn't be returning to 'normal' any time soon. As flights were by this time greatly reduced in number there were several repatriation voyages undertaken by various cruise lines.

Despite having no passengers and nowhere to go, the ships continued to have a crew presence aboard throughout the pause. This served a number of purposes. Firstly, they were required for the operation of the ship. These ships were still operating, even if they weren't going on cruises. Secondly, they performed essential maintenance tasks required to keep the ships in good condition. Thirdly, it is a requirement to have a certain number of crew aboard at all times to maintain the ship's seaworthiness certificate. As these ships were expected to return to service at some point, they needed to keep them in class so that they could return to service easily.

BIBLIOGRAPHY

Published Books

Crump, T. (2009), *A Short History of The Age of Steam*. Robinson; 1st edition.

Dawson, P. (2006), *The Liner: Retrospective and Renaissance*. W.W. Norton & Company; 1st edition.

Dawson, P. & Peter, B. (2012), *P&O at 175: A world of shipping since 1837*. Ferry Publications.

de Kerbrech, R. (2009), *Ships of the White Star Line*. Ian Allan; 1st edition.

Flounders, E. & Gallagher, M. (2014), *The Story of Cunard's 175 years: The Triumph of a Great Tradition*. Ferry Publications; 1st edition.

Frame, C. & Cross, R. (2020), *180 Years of Cunard*. The History Press; 2nd edition.

Frame, C. & Cross, R. (2013), *The Evolution of the Transatlantic Liner*. The History Press; 1st edition.

Henderson, R., Cremer, D., Frame, C. & Cross, R. (2015), *A Photographic History of P&O Cruises*. The History Press; 1st edition.

Henderson, R., Cremer, D., Frame, C. & Cross, R. (2018), *A Photographic History of The Orient Line*. The History Press; 1st edition.

Harris, C.J. & Ingpen, B.D. (1994), *Mailships of the Union-Castle Line*. Patrick Stephens Ltd.

Hill, D. & English. P. (2013), *The Great Race, The race between the English and the French to complete the map of Australia*. William Heinemann.

Hutchings, D. (2003), *Pride of the North Atlantic*. Waterfront Publications; 1st edition.

Kennedy, J. (1903), *Steam Navigation, with Numerous Illustrations*. Charles Birchall Limited.

Langley, J.G. (2002), *Steam Lion: A Biography of Samuel Cunard*. Bricktower; hardcover edition.

Lavery, B. (2010), *Ship: 5,000 years of maritime adventure*. Dorling Kindersley; 1st edition.

Miller, W. (2011), *The Last Atlantic Liners: Getting there is half the fun*. Amberley Publishing; Illustrated edition.

Preble, G.H. & Lochhead, J.L. (2018), *A Chronological History of the Origin and Development of Steam Navigation*. Palala Press; English Paperback Edition.

Talbot-Booth RNT, Pay-Lieut, E.C. (1936), *A Cruising Companion: Ships and the Sea*; 2nd Edition. D. Appleton-Century Company.

Warwick, R.W. (1999), *QE2: The Cunard Line Flagship Queen Elizabeth II*. W.W. Norton & Company.

Books printed for cruise line promotions

Author Unknown (1956), *The Great World Cruise of 1956, The Cunard Liner Caronia*. Printed in Great Britain.

Cunard Line (1997), *The Art of Cruising*. Printed in Australia.

Personal Conversations

Andrew Sassoli-Walker, personal conversations, various years.

Bill Miller, personal conversations, various years.

Dr Stephen Payne, personal conversations, various years.

Emma LeTeace, personal conversations, various years.

Rob Henderson, personal conversations, various years.

Ron Burchett, personal conversations, various years.

Articles and Newspapers

Illustrated Sydney News and New South Wales Agriculturalist and Grazier (13/07/1878), Special Correspondent. Our English Letter. p.11. Accessed in 2023 via: https://trove.nla.gov.au/newspaper/article/63335033

The Australasian Sketcher with Pen & Pencil (20/12/1897), Unspecified Author. *The Bell-Coleman Meat Preserving Process*. p.151. Accessed in 2023 via: https://trove.nla.gov.au/newspaper/page/5739934

The Sydney Morning Herald (21/09/1866), Unspecified Author. *Things worth recording about steam navigation*. p.4. Accessed in 2022 via: https://trove.nla.gov.au/newspaper/article/13137120

The Telegraph (24/05/41), Special Service. *100 million dollar convoy safely over*. p.5. Accessed in 2022 via: https://trove.nla.gov.au/newspaper/article/186643863/19742849

Websites and Digital

Bibby Line Group, *Our Story*. https://bibbylinegroup.co.uk/about/heritage (retrieved 2023).

Carrier Marine & Offshore, *Marine & Offshore History*. www.carrier.com/marine-offshore/en/worldwide/about/marine-offshore-history (retrieved 2022).

Chris' Cunard Page, *Various Pages*. www.chriscunard.com (retrieved 2022, 2023).

CNN, Samuel Pecota. *In Andrea Doria wreck, a captain who shone.* https://edition.cnn.com/2012/01/18/opinion/pecota-cruise-captain/index.html (retrieved 2022).

Company of Master Mariners of Australia. *The Black Ball Line.* www.mastermariners.org.au/stories-from-the-past/2715-the-black-ball-line (retrieved 2023).

Encyclopaedia Britannica. *History of Ships (technology).* www.britannica.com/technology/ship/History-of-ships (retrieved 2022).

Encyclopaedia Britannica. *Undersea Cable (communications).* www.britannica.com/technology/undersea-cable (retrieved 2022).

Express, Lauren Beavis & Athena Stavru. *Luxury and adventure … life on board first round the world cruise revealed.* www.express.co.uk/news/history/1641010/first-cruise-round-the-world-Phileas-Fogg-William-Alfred-Essery-SS-Ceylon (retrieved 2022).

Holland America Line, *150 Year Timeline.* www.hollandamerica.com/150th-anniversary/en/timeline (retrieved 2023).

Italian Liners Historical Society, Anthony Cooke. *Victoria.* www.italianliners.com/victoria-en (retrieved 2023).

The Last Ocean Liners, *Norwegian America Line, Oslofjord/Bergensfjord/Sagafjord.* https://lastoceanliners.com/line/norwegian-america-line/?l=NAL (retrieved 2022).

Mecaflux Heliciel. *A short history of screw propellers.* https://heliciel.com/en/Histoire-helice.htm (retrieved 2022).

Mid Ship Century, Peter Knego. *SS Carnivale.* www.midshipcentury.com/carnivale (retrieved 2023).

Mid Ship Century, Peter Knego. *MV Victoria, Lloyd Triestino.* www.midshipcentury.com/victoria-lloyd-triestino (retrieved 2022).

Mid Ship Century, Peter Knego. *SS Transvaal Castle.* www.midshipcentury.com/transvaal-castle (retrieved 2023).

Naval History and Heritage Command. *The Japanese 'Hell Ships' of World War II.* www.history.navy.mil/browse-by-topic/wars-conflicts-and-operations/world-war-ii/1944/oryoku-maru.html (retrieved 2023).

PBS, American Experience, *Wireless Signals.* www.pbs.org/wgbh/american-experience/features/rescue-wireless-signals (retrieved 2022).

People's World, Special to People's World. *This week in history: The SS Andrea Doria sinks off Nantucket.* www.peoplesworld.org/article/this-week-in-history-the-ss-andrea-doria-sinks-off-nantucket (retrieved 2022).

Royal Australian Navy, *Shipping Lists: Ormaston to Pelaw Main.* www.navy.gov.au/sites/default/files/documents/ORMISTON_TO_PELAW_MAIN.pdf (retrieved 2022).

Royal Museums Greenwich, Passenger/cargo vessel (1840); *Blackwall Frigate.* www.rmg.co.uk/collections/objects/rmgc-object-66808 (retrieved 2023).

Royal Museums Greenwich, *Robert F Stockton (1838); Passenger/cargo vessel; Steamer.* www.rmg.co.uk/collections/objects/rmgc-object-66728 (retrieved 2023).

Smithsonian, Daryl Austin, *The History of the World's First Cruise Ship Built Solely for Luxurious Travel.* www.smithsonianmag.com/history/history-worlds-first-cruise-ship-built-solely-luxurious-travel-180978254 (retrieved 2022).

State Library New South Wales, *Shipboard: the nineteenth century emigrant experience.* www.sl.nsw.gov.au/stories/shipboard-19th-century-emigrant-experience/life-board (retrieved 2022).

Stories of London, *Isambard Kingdom Brunel.* https://stories-of-london.org/isambard-kingdom-brunel-3 (retrieved 2022).

Tech Historian, Thomas Holm. *What was the first propeller driven ship?* https://techhistorian.com/first-propeller-driven-ship (retrieved 2023).

The Holland America Line Postcard Collectors Reference Library. *The Holland America Line, A History.* www.halpostcards.com/unofficial/line.html (retrieved 2023).

The National Library of New Zealand, *Various Pages.* https://natlib.govt.nz (retrieved 2022, 2023).

The Naval Historical Society of Australia, Walker Burroughs. *The Naval Evacuation of Singapore—February 1942*, Walter Burroughs. https://navyhistory.au/the-naval-evacuation-of-singapore-february-1942 (retrieved 2022).

The Only Way to Cross, Tom Hutchinson. *The Steerage Experience.* https://oceanlinersblog.wordpress.com/2018/02/11/the-steerage-experience (retrieved 2022).

The Ships List, *Various Pages.* www.theshipslist.com (retrieved 2022, 2023).

Wondrium Daily, Richard Baum, PhD. *International Exploration in the Chinese Empire: Zheng He's Voyages.* www.wondriumdaily.com/international-exploration-in-the-chinese-empire-zheng-hes-voyages (retrieved 2022).

Videos & Multimedia

Casual Navigation, *What happened to the Andrea Doria?* www.youtube.com/watch?v=rTpGjeqKtSw (viewed: 2022).

Casual Navigation, *Why are 4 Blades Better Than 3?* www.youtube.com/watch?v=2cnKzCTJC_8 (viewed: 2023).

Chris Frame Official, *Brand New Cruise Ships with Nowhere to Go!* www.youtube.com/watch?v=vnu9umQwnuE (viewed: 2022).

Chris Frame Official, *Design Secrets of Queen Mary 2 – Ocean Liner's unique features explained by Chief Naval Architect.* www.youtube.com/watch?v=d2uinSNslXo (viewed: 2022).

Chris Frame Official, *Norwegian Spirit Full HD Tour – First look after $100M refit!* www.youtube.com/watch?v=ws8XkKVAlSk (viewed: 2022).

Chris Frame Official, *Why Ocean Liners are Stronger & Faster than Cruise Ships? Key Ocean Liner Differences Explained!* www.youtube.com/watch?v=PVo08nSQ2CM (viewed: 2022).

Media Releases

Multiple media releases issued by various cruise lines.

Clockwise from top right: *Oronsay* (1925–42). The four-bladed propellers of *Oronsay* being inspected in the dry dock. (Henderson & Cremer Collection); *Caronia* (1949–67). The raked bow of *Caronia* as seen during docking manoeuvres. An officer stands at the bow to monitor the progress. (Henderson & Cremer Collection); *Queen Victoria Tender 14* (2007–). Even though many cruise ports have expanded docking facilities, cruise ships continue to utilise tenders to take passengers ashore at anchorage ports. (Frame & Cross)

ABOUT CHRIS AND RACHELLE

Chris and Rachelle have been writing maritime history books since 2008, when their first book, *QE2: A Photographic Journey*, was published. Since then, they have written and co-written over a dozen maritime history books, as well as creating a series of ocean liner colouring-in books for The History Press. Chris is a regular headline maritime history speaker at maritime museums and aboard ocean liners and cruise ships. He has a YouTube channel and is also the co-host of the popular podcast The Big Cruise Podcast.

Find Chris and Rachelle online

Stay in touch with Chris & Rachelle online at the following official channels:

Main Website: www.chrisframe.com.au
YouTube: www.youtube.com/chrisframeofficial
Cruise Merch: chrisframeofficial.teemill.com
Podcast: www.thebigcruisepodcast.com
Chris' Cunard History Website: www.chriscunard.com